The Wars Within

A. J. Perrish

The Wars Within

A. J. Perrish

XULON PRESS

Xulon Press Elite
2301 Lucien Way #415
Maitland, FL 32751
407.339.4217
www.xulonpress.com

Printed in the United States of America.

ISBN-13: 978-1-54566-263-2

Notice

This story is fiction, but these are a collection of stories from my childhood and adult life as well as friends of mine who served in the United States Marine Corp (USMC) who are no longer with us. Post-Traumatic Stress Disorder (PTSD) is real and no joking matter. We lose more veterans than we save, and this must change. PTSD comes in many shapes and forms. Veterans to civilians who have lived rough lives need our help, and we need to understand their struggle.

This book contains language and material not suitable for people under eighteen years of age unless supervised by an adult. This book also contains triggers that may cause mental issues to arise.

Please let God allow you to soak in this story and realize that you're not alone and that there is hope.

Dedication

To all the veterans we have lost in combat and to PTSD, we miss you.

To my kids: Daddy loves you. I hope this book will make you proud of your dad. I hope you learn from all my struggle in life and not repeat the same mistakes I made. It took thirty-seven years to get life right and walk the path God made for me. If there is one thing you keep in your minds and hearts in your life, it's this: *love*. Love like you will never love again. Never stop loving. Love is all we have in this world besides hope that means anything in this life. But I will warn you, love requires pain and hurt from time to time, but always look at the good that came from the loss of love. Cherish all of life. Praise God in the good and the bad. He will never leave you. I love you all.

To my ex-wives (yes, plural!): I'm sorry you had me before I got help, and I'm sorry for all the BS and lies and PTSD you had to endure. I'm sorry I grew up too late. You all gave me the best gifts in the world, *our kids*.

To Michelle, the love of my life. I never realized all these years that all the hurt and heartbreak and lessons were to teach me the true meaning of care and love. Our demons and our angels play well together. Nothing in this life will take me from you. I love you to *our* stars and back.

To Banana: You believed in me when I couldn't believe in myself and when no one else did. You fought tooth and nail to stay in my life when I was at my worst. You saw the diamond in the rough. During countless hospital stays, you held my hand, and you never failed to visit in countless mental-health wards. I'm eternally grateful and will always have a place for you in my heart. I owe you so much, and there will never be an amount of life in this body to pay you back. I know *we* didn't end like this, but I gave you the happy ending you deserved. If it wasn't for you, I couldn't have ever learned to love again. You brought my heart to life and taught me how a real relationship works and how love feels. You will forever be my Banana.

Kat Robertson: You're my backbone, my best friend, and the most beautiful redhead this world has ever seen, and I'm lucky to have you on my cover. I love you dearly.

To all my friends: Thank you for standing by me all these years and keeping me grounded when I needed it.

To AA and NA members: Keep your heads up, stay clean, and take it one day at a time.

Contents

The Dream

Location: Somewhere in the Middle East
Time: 0934

Women's screams filled the dry, stale God-forsaken air. Husbands gazed painfully upon their wives in absolute horror. Brothers and children, aunts and uncles screamed, pleading for their release and forgiveness. Fathers were forced to stand by as their daughters were tossed into an abyss of death. Evil had hit a new low in this godless desert.

A fifteen-man unit stood by, undercover, in an adjacent building. They lay in wait for their high-profile target to arrive. Due to orders they could *not* interfere with local matters no matter what was happening. These women were caught reading and had been sentenced to death and tossed into a burn pit along with their books.

Corporal Jax Guerra was a great Marine who followed orders to a "T." You'd bet your ass you'd hear about it if he didn't agree, yet he would follow his order. Corporal had only been deployed seven months at this time, still a baby at the age of twenty. The two kills he had already didn't faze him, and it seemed like nothing would.

Gunnery Sargent William Carver heads up the unit and coms the unit to stand down; no one fires a round until orders are given. Upset by this, Corporal Guerra speaks up: "Innocent women are going to die, Gunny; this is bullshit!"

"Corporal, stand down; shut your fucking mouth. I don't want any radio chatter from you," barked Gunnery Sargent Carver.

Corporal Guerra is in team two on the first floor with seven others, and team one is on the second floor with eight men.

"Fuck!" whispers Corporal Guerra. He has noticed a young boy around twelve to fourteen years old approaching with a 9mm and a soccer ball in his direction. Guerra radios his Gunny," Gunny, I have a bogey approaching the west corner, over." Gunny replies," Terminate bogey if hostile, over." "Roger that, over."

His heart starts to race, and his palms get sweaty as if it wasn't hot enough. Cpl Guerra's temperature has just increased to what feels like an extra 100 degrees. Guerra knows he can't fire, but he must disarm the boy. He quickly remembers he has a candy bar in his top right pocket. Kids there love "American" candy and fight over it. In his left hand, he holds a Butterfinger, and in his right hand, he holds his Marine Corps issued K-Bar that the corporal has spent hours sharpening and babying. The corporal hears the boy's footsteps grow closer, and his shadow peeks through the door.

All the men are frozen in position around the room with their eyes glued on the door. The boy crosses the threshold, sees one of the Marines, and rips out the 9mm from his waist and fumbles it, his fear showing brighter than the sun.

Cpl Guerra quickly makes himself visible to the boy. He holds out the candy bar, shaking like a leaf, and slowly inching forward saying, "*Khudhha, khudhha,*" meaning "take it, take it." He also whispers "shhhhh." After a standoff that felt like forever, only seventy-five seconds have passed, and Cpl and the boy are inches away from each other. The boy gently kicks his ball out of the way and inches forward and holsters his gun.

Cpl takes a deep breath and lets it out; his relief of the holstered gun makes this easier. Now all he must do is make sure the boy doesn't scream. The boy removes the candy bar from the corporal's hand. On his earpiece, Gunny is yelling for a sitrep. "Damn it, Guerra, sitrep!" One second into the boy taking the candy bar and thinking he won the lotto, Cpl. Guerra used his left hand on the skinny boy's arm in a downward motion and spins the boy around, covers the boy's mouth with his left hand, and plunges the knife in his right hand into the boy's heart.

The team looks in utter shock at what has just happened. "Sitrep, damn it, Guerra!" Gunny barks again. Still with his knife in the boy's chest as he squirms and jolts with tears down his face, Cpl drags the boy back to his original position against the wall. Fear, hate, disappointment, and thoughts of his daughter cross his mind.

Guerra's back hits the wall, and he slides down it like a sack of rocks and hits his ass in a hurry. He is fighting back tears as he hits his com line. "Bogey terminated."

"Good job, Guerra; you have secured our position."

"Copy that, Gunny."

The team stand motionless and looks on as the boy's body is still twitching and bleeding out. Cpl Guerra lets a tear fall but doesn't acknowledge it as he slowly pulls the knife out of the boy's chest cavity. He pushes the boy off himself and crawls over to the candy bar and places it back into his pocket right next to the picture of his kid. Drenched in a kid's blood was the last thing his day would include, but war is new for the corporal, and anything is now possible. The corporal thought his day couldn't get any worse, but in the distance, a big rig can be heard getting closer and closer.

The teams are drawn to a horrific sight of a gas tanker arriving on site. The screams turn into begging and pleading. One father begs at the feet of one of the terrorist's feet. The terrorist unloads three rounds into the head of the father, and his limp body flies back and hits the ground as his brain matter paints the wall behind him.

A man hops out of the truck and connects a hose to the back valve and turns a knob. The hose fills up with not just gas, but death. He walks to the pit with the other end of the fire hose and looks to the man in charge. The head of this evil snake barks an order, and the piece of shit holding the hose turns the handle on the hose, and gasoline spews out.

"Gunny, we can't let this go down!"

"Corporal, shut the fuck up—maintain radio silence. I don't need you blowing our op for a few women. We cannot act in local matters!"

After a few minutes, the man shuts the valve off and rolls up the hose and heads back to the front of the pit. He yells something indistinct and looks toward a man who looks like he is running things. This man stands on a roof across from the pit as if it's his throne. The man in charge motions to the man who was pouring gas, and he pulls a flare out of his pocket. He lights it and raises his hand in the air and yells, "*Almot ali alkvar!*"

The gas fumes ignite and sends the man flying back and in flames. The women's screams and the sound of the explosion could be heard for miles. Jax Guerra wakes up screaming in his bed two minutes before his alarm is set to go off. Jax sits up, dripping sweat and breathing heavily.

"One more night, same bad dream, fuck my life."

The Reality

Looking as if he just ran a 10k marathon, Jax peeled off his sheets and swung his legs off the edge of the bed. He sat there and looked to his left and stared at his nightstand as if it held the answer to all his prayers and pain. Jax leaned over and reached over to the handle of the top drawer. He opened the drawer, and something caught his eye. Intensely, he gazed inside of it. He reached into the drawer and pulled out his 9mm handgun. It was shiny and perfectly clean as he cleaned it almost two times a week after his travels to the range where he blew off some steam. He gazed at it and felt the weight of it in his hands.

For the three hundred and second time Jax places the barrel of the gun inside his mouth and aims it to the back of his throat. He feels the coldness of the steel as his mouth closes around the barrel. His teeth chatter on the unforgiving metal, and a single tear falls from his eye.

Suddenly, he sees his daughter standing at his bedroom door, her long blonde hair flowing and bright blue eyes staring deep into his, and she has the most beautiful smile he has ever seen. He quickly pulls the gun out of his mouth and looks back at the door, and she is gone. He places the gun back into his drawer and slams it shut. Jax remembers the kids are at their mom's house, so he once again he is having a slight hallucination.

Jax stands up and the sweat runs down his chest and abs like they are rolling over small hills in the Napa Valley. Jax, being divorced and the kids not being at home, he has no issue with walking around in his boxer briefs and nothing else. He stretches and grabs his lower region and adjusts himself accordingly. He heads to the kitchen, and two steps out his bedroom door, his alarm sounds off. He jumps through the roof and scares the hell out of himself. He turns around and shuts off the alarm clock that he swears will get tossed out the damn window one of these days.

He realizes that he did his daughter's famous eye roll when he shut it off and couldn't believe his teenage daughter was rubbing off on him. He chuckled as he thought about what was next—his daughter's

"OMG" line, or maybe he would start biting his nails nervously.

Jax now slowly stumbles down the hallway and enters the kitchen. He opens the fridge and pulls out his favorite Italian creamer and heads for the coffee pot. He then sees he didn't set the timer so there is no coffee. He is stopped in his tracks. He jokingly says "OMG" like his daughter and grabs the unfortunately empty coffeepot, fills it with water, walks over to the coffee maker, and pours the water into it.

He opens the cabinet above the maker and reaches in and grabs the coffee container, and he stops dead in his tracks once again. He stares at the coffee container. His coffee container is plastic and lightweight, but with coffee in it, it is rather heavy. But in this case, it is extremely light. He slowly pulls it out of the cabinet and slowly peels off the lid. To his horror, it is bone dry. Nothing, not even enough to make one half cup.

Jax leaves it all on the counter and heads to his protein powder and makes his shake as usual, but this time he makes it violently and shakes it as if it stole his bike as a kid. He grabs a spoon to scrape off the foam he so despises. While doing so, he drops the spoon, and it crashes to the ground, not only making one hell of a crash, but spewing the foam all over the floor.

Again, Jax jumps and get startled. His heart races and his forehead start to bead up with sweat. Shaking it off, Jax grabs his No-Xplde pre-workout mix and makes a quick drink and slams it as if it was old olive oil his mom made him drink. Not that it tastes bad; he loves the taste but loves to drink it as a shot.

About ten paces to his weight room he realized he turned into his daughter and just stomped away from his coffeepot. He shakes his head and continues to his weight room. Jax loves his weight room. It's not his hobby; it's his lifestyle and routine that eight years in the Marines instilled in him.

After a grilling, two-hour workout, Jax heads to his second-favorite room of his house: the bathroom. Jax remodeled his house on his own and loves it. He spent extra time and care, though, on his bathroom; no expense was too much or too little. Jax turns on his "fancy" shower as his daughter puts it. The twenty heads fire up, and the rainmaker overhead showerhead starts to pour. Jax takes a quick pee and drops his drawers.

Jax presses some of the buttons and CMT pops on with their morning videos and soothing country twang, which makes Jax feel like he is home back on base. It's an epic experience to have and, well, also the view is nice. Jax just stands there letting the water drain and glide over his perfectly sculpted chest, abs, and ass.

A news update breaks on his TV, and of course it's about the Middle East, and because he has already had enough about the Middle East this morning, he shuts off his TV and continues with a brief wash off and gets out of the shower.

Jax knows it's going to be a long day. All he must do is make it through until he gets his babies. Nothing gets in the way of him seeing his kids, and he knows once he has them, he will be okay.

He decides that a walk to his coffee spot is required this morning, but he is rather too jumpy to drive. Plus, a thirty-minute walk wouldn't kill him and would be the perfect opportunity to have his headphones on and observe the surroundings. After two lights taking their sweet time and a school bus loading a child, he has finally made it to the coffee shop where his life and day will be taking some unexpected turns.

The Coffee Shop

Jax walks into the Campbell Coffee Company where he had been a regular for nine years. The line, as usual, is back to the door, and the baristas are running all over the place, filling coffee and pastry orders, but the main thing they serve in the morning is their signature breakfast sandwich.

Jax passed by the line and went straight to the pickup counter to a beautiful redhead who has eyes that pierce his soul every time he investigates hers.

"Good morning, Marine."

Jax smiles back and looks back at her. "Not as good as that smile, Banana." He tosses her a bigger smile and a wink. Jax walks away to his regular table. Shanna not only is Jax's best friend but also the coffee shop owner. After snagging his table, he walks back up to Shanna as she has his sandwich ready for him. Jax is aware of the flirting that goes on between them, but he does not know how deep that goes. He is rather dense when it comes to the opposite sex. Jax reaches up.

"Thanks, Hun."

His hand grazes hers and he takes the plate. All she can do is giggle and blush right now this early in the morning. Shanna turns even redder than her hair, and her knees are about to buckle. She pretends to faint like a star-struck high school teenager, directed at one of her close employees.

"You looooveee him!!!"

Shanna pushes her employee, and they both laugh. "Shut up or you're fired!"

Shanna walks back to her office and takes a breath. She has just as much love for her shop as she does for its customers. She has poured her heart and soul into it and yearns for someone to share it with.

Jax sits at his favorite table with a view of the doors and exits and his back to the wall. He is relaxing and enjoying his chai and sandwich just like he does every morning. Just then there is a loud slamming of a crash ten feet away from Jax which send his coffee and half his sandwich flying across the shop. This usually doesn't occur when Jax is around for the newspaper delivery in the morning, but Louis was running late today. Highway 85 is known for its ridiculous accidents, and today caused a two-hour delay in everything and set forth the unfortunate crashing of a newspaper stack.

Beads of sweat start to build up on Jax's forehead like a morning dew on a foggy bay area morning. All his nervous ticks are starting to show, fingers tapping, leg shaking, and a slight twitch in his neck. All the worst is starting to come out.

The Best Friends

Shanna comes out from the back and motions for Jax to join her outside for their ritual smoke, which they really need to quit. They hear it enough from the whole town! It is perfect timing for Jax; some outside air could do him some good. His anxiety is through the roof, and he needs a smoke. His coffee and sandwich are being remade for him, and he reaches the door to walk out with Shanna.

Jax places his hand at the lower area of her back and guides her through the door. Shanna loves the gentleman side of Jax. He is everything she looks for in a man, and she has completed her checklist for a man on him. She loves his six-foot, 250-pound stature. His brown hair makes his eyes pop even harder with their deep sea-green finish. The tattoos push her over the edge; they gave him the rough and rugged bad boy look, when he is such a sweetheart and a family man.

She also loves his heart. He is an advocate for abused children and is a recovering addict. The biggest plus to Jax is his heart for God. He prays before meals, never misses his men's prayer team on Wednesdays, and is always there at church without failure on Sundays. She has been a little flirtier since he grew the beard out.

Shanna pulls out a cigarette of her pack and offers one to Jax as he shakes his head.

"Girl, you know I only smoke Camels."

She chuckles. "I figured one day you'll turn into a real man and smoke Marlboro. "

He just shakes his head at her and pulls a cig out of his pack and lights hers, then his.

Jax inhales and takes in a nice, long drag that billows out a humongous cloud of smoke. Shanna looks to him and knows something isn't right. She hasn't heard a sigh like that since the divorce.

"Shanna, let me ask you something."

Jax pauses. Shanna turns to face him.

Shanna speaks up, "Oh, here comes the bad news."

Shanna leans her head back. Jax places his hand on her shoulder and moves in closer.

"Do you, have a fix-it" list?

"Yes" she responds with a puzzled look on her face but enjoying his hand on her. "Why do you ask?" She takes another drag and exhales.

Jax moves his hand lower, knowing exactly what he is doing. "Banana, I need to stay busy, and your fix-it list will let me stay busy until I get the kids. And you get to spend the day with me."

She looks at Jax like a deer caught in the headlights and just shaking her head yes. The only sound she can get out is mumbled "Ummhmm" as he rubs her back.

"Whatever you want, Jax," finally spills out.

Jax stops rubbing her back and starts to walk away. He turns, smiles at her, and walks back into the shop.

Shanna realizes her lower womanly area has started reacting in the most inopportune time and pulsing to her heartbeat. She puts out her cigarette. "I should have worn a pad for today!" she sighs and walks back into the shop.

She walks back up to Jax. "After nine years, you offer help in the shop. Why? What's going on?" She stands there with her hands on her hips as if she is demanding an answer, but he see her as such a cutie that he can't take her seriously.

He reaches for her belt loop and tries to pull her closer to hug her because he will get his way. She slaps his hand and asks again. He smiles and just replies, "Nothing." And he began looking at his phone.

She plants her foot and says, "Fine, you can do the list, but I get dinner at your place if you do it!"

Jax looks to her and replies, "You know that won't happen. Alexis will shit a brick." He looks at her with that look of "you know better than to ask."

She spins around walks away. "Okay, how about I come down with the kids later, and we all get ice cream?"

She spins around starts to walk away again, making a smiley face to her employees with a tremendous giddy smirk. She spins back around with a serious look on her face and agrees, "Deal!" She spins playfully around and skips to the back of the shop and disappears.

BOOM! A loud bang that sounded like gun fire rips through Jax's ears, and he hits the floor. What seemed so innocent to everyone else as a car backfiring was a horrible trigger for Jax. His anxiety is growing, and he doesn't know how much more he can take. What looked like Campbell had turned into a flashback for Jax. What he sees is no longer Campbell. He sees the streets of Baghdad in June. Jax doesn't believe what he sees. He gets to his knees, covers his eyes, and counts to ten like he was taught to do. He reopens his eyes, and he is safely back in the coffee shop. Jax doesn't know it yet, but this is just the beginning.

Jax goes outside to get some air and have a smoke to calm his nerves. Jax was thinking way too much. "This list may not have what it takes to keep me sane. Get it together Jax; you got this."

Jax takes off his jacket and places it on the arm of a chair outside. He pulls out his phone and scrolls to Gunny Carver. He presses send, paces the sidewalk, and waits for the gunny to answer. To this day he can't understand why he has such a horrible Taylor Swift ringtone. What's even worse, Jax catches himself humming to it and abruptly stops when Gunny answers the line.

"Jax! What's up? No wait let me guess, Campbell coffee? See you in ten."

Master Gunnery Sargent William Carver, one of the best friends and best Marines to have on your six, sounds off through the phone, which he still treats like it's a com line.

"Just hurry, Will."

"Jax, you okay?

"Gunny, just get your ass here!"

"Copy that, out."

Jax hangs up and turns around. He sees Shanna looking at him, smiling from inside. She is just staring and rocking back and forth as if they are dancing together.

"Hey, Boss, you okay?" Shanna's employee asks.

"Just imagining Jax dancing with me."

"You're dick-whooped, and he hasn't given it to you yet."

"Shut up or you're fired!" Shanna laughs and starts to walk away.

"That's the second time today you tried to fire me." The employee smirks and flips her hair.

Shanna laughs flips her hair back at her and follows Jax over to his table.

The List

As Jax opens the door, he is greeted by Shanna, galloping over to him. He places his hand on the small of her back, and they walk to Jax's table. She spins around quickly and has an enormous smile on her face. She loves when Jax touches her lower back and is energized by it. Jax, with a worried look on his face, tries to smile, but it comes out looking more like a half-assed smile while being constipated.

"So, Marine, here is the list!" She is bouncing like a little girl getting a reward. Her giddy and giggly tone make him crack a smile of amusement.

Shanna places her arm around Jax and walks him to the back.

As they walk, he says, "This is some list, hon." Jax looking at the list with wide-open eyes as if he has just realized what he got himself into.

They arrive to the back closet, and she releases Jax and faces him.

"Don't judge me, Jax." Shanna opens the door and the only thing that Jax thinks to himself was, *Holy little baby Jesus, that's a mess and a half.*

"Banana, how is this whole place on point, but when you get the actual cleaning closet, it's a disaster?" Jax laughs and shakes his head. Shanna turn three shades of red.

"It's a work in progress . . ." Shanna stands there looking like a five-year-old who just shoved all her dirty clothes under her bed. Jax looks at Shanna and places his hand on her shoulder.

"Banana, a work in progress I can believe, yet a good start is throwing it all away and starting over, babe."

Shanna bites her lower lip and tosses Jax a half-cocked smile and giggles in embarrassment.

Jax ducks and twitches to the sound of a loud bang from outside. Shanna looks at him puzzled and asks if he is okay, but he blows it off as if something flew in his ear. He is the best at deflection and changing the subject to any conversation. But with this, he couldn't hide the worried look on his face.

Shanna places her hand on his chest and looks him dead in the eyes. "Jax, are you okay?" She steps in closer and struggles to make eye contact with Jax. A booming voice sounds off as Jax starts to speak. "You two decent?" A laugh roars out as a huge man walks around the corner; it's William.

"Well, Jax looks heinous, but Shanna, you're looking gorgeous as ever!" William flirts, Shanna rolls her eyes, and Jax shakes his head and places his hand on William's shoulder.

"Shut up, Will; I will get your coffee."

"Thanks, doll, you're terrific!" William laughs.

Shanna sticks out her tongue and walks to the front. Jax laughs. "Dude, you're always hitting on her and getting the same reaction." They both laughed and shrugged it off and headed to the front of the café. "So, you look like hell, Jax." Jax looks to William and motions for him to follow him outside to smoke.

As they walk past the front counter, Jax tosses a wink at Shanna. Her employee notices and smiles as she is making the next cup of coffee. "I bet you were wearing a pad, weren't you?" Shanna looks at her in shock, then a few seconds later starts to laugh and walks to the back office. Her employee is impressed with herself and that comment, but all Shanna could think of was that she was totally right.

Jax and William light up their cigarettes. William sits in the chair on the patio and looks up to Jax. "What's the problem, brother?" William asked with a bit of concern in his tone.

Jax leans against the wall and takes a long drag off his smoke. "I'm having flashbacks, hearing and seeing shit that isn't really there." Jax exhales and pulls another drag of cold-blooded nicotine.

William sits back and exhales deeply. He looks to Jax and says, "Oh man, Jax, do you want to go to the VA now or later?"

Jax quickly replies "No!"

"Bro, you need meds and help," William stated, concerned.

"No, it'll pass. I will stay busy with Banana's list, and then I'll have the kids."

William stands up, adjusts his pants, and faces Jax. "Dude, I need you to track me real good—you cannot snap in public again. It's not safe for you or anyone else." William takes a few steps back and turns around breathing heavily while stressing out. "Fuck the list; you need help. Don't make me call your mom, Bro."

Jax comes off the wall, squares up with William, and crosses his arms. Jax squints, cocks his head to the left, and stares at William. With his intense stare, he leans his head back and mutters, "You wouldn't."

William squares up and crosses his arms and with the same stare and mutters, "Yes, I will," and ends the statement with an evil smile.

Jax unfolds his arm and steps in closely to William. "Before you say anything, Jax, I outrank you, I'm twice your size, and you are just attached to my unit. I've got your momma on speed dial. Get your shit in line and unfuck yourself real quick."

Jax hears Shanna's voice and turns to see her coming. He quickly turns to William. "Shanna is coming; just shut the fuck up. I don't want her to know."

William glares at him and frowns, crossing his arms once again.

Shanna plowed through the door with a slight stumble with joyful swagger, gallivants down the ramp, and hands William his coffee. "That's five-fifty," Shanna states with a shit-eating grin. William looks at the coffee cup, looks at Shanna, looks back at the coffee cup, and then looks back at Shanna. Looking puzzled, William dumbfoundedly asks, "Why five fifty? That's two dollars more than yesterday." Still puzzled, Williams still looks at her in shock as Shanna walks away.

She turns with a smile "Guess you won't be calling me Doll again." Shanna continues to walk away as she and Jax laugh about the look on William's face. Also William has just realized he gave Shanna a ten and won't get his change back.

After a brief comedown of recent events, Williams gets his bearings back, looks to Jax, and says, "So when are you two going to hook up and throw Alexis to the proverbial curb?"

Shanna walks down the ramp notices William smiling with his hand on Jax's shoulder. She realizes Jax is beet red. Shanna walks up and gives William his change, and he looks at the dollar bill like its foreign money.

"Where is the rest of it?"

Shanna smirks and says, "You were a good tipper today. Emily says "Thank you." Shanna looks at Jax and notices he is still beet red, with beads of sweat dripping down his forehead. "Jax, what's wrong?"

Jax can't make eye contact. It seems like the ground has become more interesting, and he feels like he's back in tenth grade, about to ask his crush to the dance.

William perks up "Oh, I just asked him when you two were gonna hook up and kick Alexis to the curb . . . So he's mad . . ."

"You're an ass hat," Shanna spats. Shanna looks down in embarrassment.

Jax looks up and says "So . . . the Dodgers just clinched their fifth NL West pennant." Jax smiles and puts his hands on his hips, knowing he just punched William right in between the eyes because he's a Giants fan. Williams shouts out a fuck you, but Jax's plan backfired, for Shanna is a Giants fan, too. She reached back and punched Jax playfully in the stomach. William and Shanna both walk away and head back into the café. Jax, overly happy with that interaction, lights up another cigarette. There is one thing that Jax loves more than the Dodgers—pissing off Giants fans. After a brief celebratory cigarette Jax walks back inside. Shanna is back behind her bar. Jax tosses a wink as usual, but this time she just glares back at him.

The Girlfriend and the Mother

William is sitting at Jax's table as Jax walks up. William leans back in his chair and places his hands behind his head. "Where is the dumb blonde this morning? She's usually making my life hell by now."

Jax rolls his eyes and sighs out loud, "Working out, yoga, then here. It's Friday, Will."

William leans forward, places one elbow on the table, and points at Jax. "You know, Bro, you're kind of a dick. Always parading Alexis in front of Shanna. You know that poor girl has been in love with you for years."

Jax just crosses his arms and breathes. They have this conversation every day. Jax digs into his daughter's bag of tricks and pulls out the teenager eye roll as he looks at William. "Bro, you need to chill. I have bigger issues right now."

William crosses his arms leans back and says, "I know. I'm just saying, Bro. If you swap them out, you're getting like free coffee for life."

Jax cuts William off. "Dude, enough!"

"Okay fine. So what's the plan? VA? Metal health clinic? Weed? Oh, please say weed first."

Jax gives William the evil eye. "No, fix-it list."

Jax gets up and walks to the back. Jax tries one last time walking past the coffee counter and throws one last wink at Shanna who had returned from yoga. Shanna melts and giggles. "Shit, Jax, knock it off. I'm mad at you!"

"Not anymore, Banana." Jax smiles and throws another wink and heads to the back.

William now sits alone at the table. He leans back into his chair and puts his feet up on another chair while placing his hands behind his head. "Sure, Jax, I'll sit here all by myself and wait for the devil . . . alone . . . I'm so scared." William chuckles to himself and glances down at his left arm, and says, "Oh the chills; my spider sense is tingling. She is close." William takes another sip of expresso, "The Taliban, no problem. Al-Qaeda, no problem. South American rebels, chill. Alexis? Scary as shit!"

As Jax is walking to the back, he realizes a huge problem. With every other step he takes, his vision changes. With one step, he's in his jeans and tennis shoes, but with every other step, it's a different world. The tile is now sand. His tennis shoes have become door kickers, and his pants have become BDUs soaked in blood. Jax stops after a couple dozen paces and finally looks down again. All he sees is blood everywhere on the ground. "*Fuck,*" he thinks. He shuts his eyes and counts to ten and starts his tapping procedures. After a few minutes, he reopens his eyes, and everything is back to normal.

Shanna follows him after seeing this. She walks up to Jax at the cleaning closet. "Jax, are you sure you're okay? What I just witnessed is not being okay."

"I'm fine, Shanna. I just need to get busy."

Shanna smirks, "I wish." Shanna walks away but stands around the corner to watch. Jax breathes in deeply and holds it. He stands there rubbing his eyes and breathes out, and luckily everything looks normal. All Shanna can do is wonder what's eating at him, and all she knows that she can do is worry.

After a few minutes, Jax uncovers his face and exhales as he tries to fight back tears as he hears the women's screaming echo ominously from that day.

Shanna quickly walks up. "Jax, what is really going on? You're not acting right one bit."

Shanna places her hand on his shoulder, and Jax takes a deep breath and replies, "I'm having some mental issues today. It's not a big deal." Jax tries to smile, but the stress is written all over his face as tears well up. At this point Jax is ready to snap even though it's been years since this has happened.

Shanna throws her arms around Jax, "Oh, Jax, I'm so sorry." Shanna tears up, "What can I do?"

Gripping tighter and tighter, Shanna finally loosens her grip when Jax finally replies, "I just need to work, Banana. William is staying close to keep an eye out."

"I'm worried, Jax. If you need to leave, just go and let me know, okay?" Shanna once again tightened her grip.

A high-pitched "Eew" comes from behind them, and Shanna lets go of Jax. Jax wipes his eyes and sees his girlfriend Alexis standing behind them. "Thanks, Banana." Jax turns and faces Alexis and greets her with a "Hi, Baby. Coffee, please, Coffee Girl." Alexis laughs as if it's just a joke, but Alexis truly hates Shanna with a passion, just as Shanna hates Alexis.

Jax and Alexis have been a "thing" for four years and counting. Jax still won't pop "The Question." They make the perfect Californian couple. Jax being a Marine and weighing in at 250 pounds, with 9 percent body fat, and chiseled like a Greek god, with light brown hair and soul-searching green eyes. He stands at six feet tall. If his eyes and smile don't get your attention, his tattoos that cover 90 percent of his body will.

Alexis, on the other hand, is your classic Californian blonde bombshell—foot ten inches tall, blue eyes, with an hourglass figure. Of course, fake as all hell. Fake tan, fake tits, fake Brazilian butt, all held together by anorexia and way too much caffeine and yoga every day. The comparison between Alexis and Shanna is staggering.

Shanna stands five foot eight, her hair a golden fire-engine red that could set California ablaze. Her eyes are like perfect sapphires of piercing hazel blue. Her skin is like a porcelain doll with flushed cheeks and perfect pouty lips. She's a wild, pure soul. Unlike Alexis, all of Shanna curves are real and natural, a perfect 10 woman with the heart to match. It matches Jax's teddy bear side only a select few have seen.

Alexis snarls at Jax, "Jax, pick up my coffee and bring it to our table." Jax sighs. Shanna retorts in a vexed manner, "I know, I know, Jax. Zebra mocha with spit . . . I mean, with whip cream."

Jax looks deep into Shanna's eyes with the stare of a father, leans forward, squints his eyes, and says sternly, "Behave." Shanna playfully smiles as she walks away to go make the drink. Jax walks around the corner and onward to his table. He starts to pass Shanna and hears her faintly coughing up a lougie. Jax quickly leans over the counter, peers around the coffee machine, smiles, and looks to Shanna. "I'm watching you." Jax leans back and continues to walk toward the table as Shanna gives him a dirty look and sticks her tongue out in defiance. Jax sees Alexis standing by William at the table. All that comes to his mind is, "Oh shit. Here we go again." Jax reaches the table. He lightly caresses the small of Alexis's back as she turns toward him.

As Alexis turns, she notices Shanna watching them. Alexis threw her arms around Jax, kissed his neck, and said loudly—just loud enough for Shanna to hear—"I missed you, baby. Kiss momma!" Alexis corners Jax and kisses him on the lips. Jax isn't one for PDA, so she knows she only has a moment to prove that Jax is hers. Alexis opens her eyes and winks at Shanna. Shanna storms off to get fresh whip cream.

"Okay, okay." Jax tries to push Alexis off. "Too mushy, babe," he tells her. "Babe you know better."

Alexis takes a step back and intertwines their fingers together and looks at the floor like a child getting into trouble. "Sorry, Jax, I've just missed you a lot is all." She looks up at him like a wounded puppy dog.

Jax grabs his chair, pulls it out, and tells Alexis to just sit down. Just as Jax's butt hits the wood of the chair, Alexis's coffee is ready. Jax used his daughter's famous eye roll, stood up, and headed to the pickup window. Shanna extends her arm while making another spitting sound. Jax reaches out and grabs the cup of coffee while gently touching Shanna's hand in the exchange. Shanna melts. Jax gives her a gentle smile and returns to his table.

Jax hands Alexis her coffee. "Thank you!" Alexis says in an overexaggerated joyous tone. She gives William a dirty look and takes a sip of her coffee. An evil laugh from the back office rings in the air, making Alexis think Shanna did something to her coffee.

Alexis crosses her legs and places her hand on top of her knee and holds her coffee, "So, Jax, I have a really good question for you." Now because of her tone, he knows it's going to be about Shanna. Alexis faces Jax as she taps her mug.

"Before you go there, Alexis, I've had a horrible morning, and I don't need you yelling at me." Jax pulls out a cigarette and holds one out for William. As William takes a cigarette, he whispers into Jax ear, “It’s a trap, Jax; be careful. I’ve seen this on *National Geographic,* and the men always die.” William pulls away laughing.

“Sweetie, why were you two hugging?” Alexis asks.

“See, Babe, that’s a problem. I say I’ve had a horrible morning, and you’re more concerned with an innocent hug.” Jax stands up and places his cigarette in his mouth, “Will, let’s smoke.” Will stands up and follows Jax to the door. “Jax, don’t walk away from me—answer my purely innocent question.” Alexis stands up.

Jax stops at the door and turns, looking down at the floor and slowly looking up to Alexis. “I’ll hug my friends, and they will hug me if they want. It’s called compassion, Alexis.” Jax reaches up and wraps his arm around William’s shoulder, “See? A hug.” Jax and William both laugh and walk out the door. Alexis stomps her foot and sits down with a pout.

William and Jax stand outside smoking, horsing around as usual, when a familiar voice sounds off from behind them.

“J, I though you quit smoking?” Jax turns around with a huge smile. There stands a brunette, roughly mid-sixties, in a dress fit for church. Diamonds and pearls drip from her neck and hands. She walks with elegance and oozes Southern charm. She's the type of woman who light up any room she walks into. He smile is as infectious as a common cold. Jax runs up and picks her up and spins her around. Shanna bears witness to one of Jax tender moments and wishes he would spin her around like that one day.

"Mom, what are you doing?"

"Getting coffee, dear. What does it look like?"

"I've missed you."

"I can tell by all the messages you have left."

"I'm sorry, Mom; I'll call more. I've been really busy. I may even stop by." Jax wipes away a tear from his eye.

Jax's foster mom peers around and sees through the window that a certain blonde is sitting at the table. "I see that trollop is still around." Joleen rolls her eyes and looks back to Jax.

"Mom, stop. I get it enough from everyone else."

"I'm sorry, my dear. I just don't know why you date her when Shanna is purely in love with you. It just makes sense."

William raises his hand and high-fives Joleen for her award-winning statement.

"Look, you two. I'm reevaluating our relationship as we speak. Four years is a long time to walk away from."

"Fair enough, J." Joleen steps in close and places both hands on his chest and pats him. Jax puts his arm around her shoulders. "Just don't take too long, son. You know I love you and only want the best for you." Joleen stops and investigates Jax face.

"J, what's wrong? Your eyes are screaming that you're in pain."

"Damn, Bro, even your mom can tell." William laughs and completely stops by the glance given by Joleen. William throws his hands up and walks back to the door and walks inside.

"Your foster dad had the same look for years, God rest his soul. Just don't follow in his footsteps, my love." Tears form in her eyes as she remembers her husband, who took his own life after suffering from PTSD from the Vietnam War.

"I won't, Momma," he replies.

"Good! Coffee time." Joleen walks inside.

Jax stands outside, not knowing how to feel or think. William walks back outside.

"Sorry to split, but that mom look Jojo has is scaring me."

"Gunny, you have been through two wars, nine deployments, and remember you did that nine-month prisoner exchange at GITMO? And you're afraid of all women?" Jax laughs and walks inside away from William.

"They're all scary." William gets goosebumps and shivers as if someone has walked over his grave. William hurries inside. "Hey wait up."

Alexis storms past William, "Bye, Alexis." William tried to be nice, but all he got was Alexis's middle finger. William sits at the table next to Jax.

"Tornado JoJo got her to leave?" Will asks.

"Yup. In record time, too," Jax answers. Jax zones out watching his foster mom talk to Shanna. Wondering how different life would be if he was with someone his family loved and respected. Shanna and Joleen give one final embrace as Joleen pays for her coffee and joins Jax and William.

The Butterfinger

Jax, William, and Shanna all waved bye to Joleen as she drove away. Shanna asked, "Which foster mom was Joleen?"

"Forty," replied Jax.

"Besides my adoptive parents, she was my favorite." Jax looked off in the distance as if a bad movie of a beating from Joleen's husband played in his head.

Williams snapped his fingers in Jax's face. "Hey, get out of there," William yelled.

"Anyways, she's my favorite," said Shanna.

"That's because you've never met my adoptive mom."

"I would have loved that." Shanna smiled at Jax and placed her hand on his shoulder and then walked inside.

William stepped up. "Look, Jax, I know it's July. July is hard for all of us, but you got to get help."

"I will," Jax replied. "Do you even remember why July is hard for me, Gunny?" Jax asked.

"I know it was one of our first deployments together and one of your most deadly months," William stated.

"It was, yes. But none of that gets to me. It's that one . . . that one that haunts me every single day. The kid." Jax slouched.

"Oh shit, Bro, I totally forgot about that. I was on the team upstairs, and you were downstairs on team two. That's when we learned to never lay a finger on your Butterfinger." Williams laughed as Jax threw a hard right punch into Williams arm.

"Damn it, Will!" Jax yelled.

"I'm serious." William laughed harder. Jax sat down on the curb. William sat next to him.

"I can still smell the burn pit, I can still hear all those women screams. I used to think I'd wake up from their screams being so loud until Jen told me it was my screaming that wakes me up."

"Jax, Jesus, man. You got to go in today," William solemnly said as he wrapped one arm around Jax.

"I remember shaking to death when the boy was about ready to take the candy bar. He looked just as scared as I was. The look on his face and the sigh of relief as he took the candy bar for some reason told me to grab him. I yanked his arm down, so it would spin him around and cover his mouth. I had gloves on, so when he bit down on my finger, it didn't hurt as bad. He smelled really bad for a kid, like a year of gym clothes and sweat. He kicked and elbowed me as we struggled. My right hand felt his ribs break, and I could hear him scream and cry as my blade cuts into his chest. He was so thin the blade poked though him almost an inch out of his back. I dragged him back to the wall because I was about to lose it. When my back hit the wall, I collapsed to the ground; I couldn't even stand up. All my energy was used to keep the kid quiet and hold him from thrashing around. I don't know how long it took for his frail body to stop twitching. That's when I commed you for sitrep. I pushed the kid off and gathered myself. I picked up the Butterfinger and placed it next to my kid's photo in my pocket."

A tear flowed down both their cheeks as the story unfolded. William had never heard this story before. No one would talk about it. Just that it was some brutal shit. Jax and William sit in silence.

The Lunch

After a brief heart-to-heart, Will takes off to run some errands while Jax heads inside to put in some work, plus Shanna is swamped for lunch hour.

The first couple of tasks seemed easy enough, so Jax went to every door and tightened all the loose screws and hinges.

Next on the list is the broken and loose chair stack. Jax spends the next fifteen minutes tightening all the loose chairs and places to one side three broken chairs that need glue and missing screws.

After spending thirty minutes looking for wood glue. Jax retires that idea and decides to walk to the hardware store a few short blocks away.

While out, Jax realized how busy Shanna was and figured she didn't eat lunch. He rolls into the sushi joint on his way back and ordered Shanna all her favorites. For starters, he got her miso soup, followed by some tempura veggies, some spicy tuna hand roll, and a firecracker roll.

For himself, he went to Subway next door. Jax loves sushi, but he wants it to be special treat just for her. Plus, he knows he will eat whatever she won't since she hates leftovers.

It seems like the perfect time for a break—just right timing as Jax walks back into the coffee shop and the last customer is served. Jax walks over to his table. Shanna noticing Jax return, and she skips like a little girl over to Jax.

While on her way, a regular customer makes a remark, "'bout time, you two." Shanna quickly retorts, "Shut it, Gladys!" as she skips by.

"What you got in the bags, Marine?" she curiously asks.

"Well, Banana, first off I have wood glue and screw for your chairs."

"Okay," she giggles.

"Next, I have Subway for me," he slowly murmurs.

"And for me?" she pines, noticing the bag that says "SUSHI."

"Well, Banana, I have miso soup." Jax smiles.

"That's it," he adds, and she punches him.

"What else, jerk?"

"Since you're so sweet, I got you veggie tempura, firecracker roll, and spicy tuna and rolls!"

"You got all my favorites, Marine! You know me too well." She is giddy with excitement. She turns to get silverware. Jax stops her.

"And so there's no dishes, I got all we need here. So sit down." Jax snaps his fingers and points to her chair. Jax also is smiling as if he knows he scored major points. Shanna sits down.

"And what did you get from Subway?"

"Everything but cucumbers, salt, pepper, oil, and vinegar. Boom! Like a boss!" Jax is thoroughly excited and proud of himself.

"Why didn't you get sushi for you, hon?" Shanna queries.

"It's a treat just for you. Wanted to make you feel special."

"Aw, thanks, sweetie." Shanna stands up walks over to Jax and gives him a hug. They both sit back down and start to eat, and Shanna mixes her wasabi and soy sauce together.

"Jax, hon, what's eating at you? And don't tell me nothing 'cause I know you!" demands Shanna. Jax looks down, not knowing how to answer this question. He doesn't want her to think he is a monster or a murderer. He also doesn't want to lie since she knows when he is lying. He also feels stuck and doesn't know what to do.

"Back in 2003, William and I were deployed together, as you already know." Jax takes a deep pausing breath. "We had a very rough day on July 18, and that's tomorrow. So it was a bad day that resurfaces almost every day since then, and today is the worst it's ever been." Jax exhales and lowers his head.

Shanna moved her chair closer and grabbed Jax's hand. "Jax, it's okay. My stepfather deals with PTSD. It's okay." Shanna rubs his hand with hers. "I minored in abnormal psychology because of him. Just know you're not alone, okay, Marine?"

"Yes, Banana. I'm sorry; you must think I'm broken now," Jax mumbled.

"No, sir, I do not!" Shanna says forcefully.

"The flashbacks are getting bad. William will take me in if it gets worse," states Jax.

"Look, hon, we are here for you and the kids. We can help as much as you need, okay?" Shanna rubs Jax back and holds his hand. "Jax you'll be okay. You know we love you and the kids, and if you need help for a bit, we can watch them."

"No, it's fine. I know they love you, too. We all do. But the VA just shoves pills at you."

"That's not true, Jax. You just have to give them a chance," she replies.

"Oh yeah? You all love me?"

Shanna laughed. Jax looks deep into her eyes as if he sees her in a different light.

"Yes, we do," she says in a low hypnotizing voice. Jax smiles, reaches into his pocket, and tells Shanna to go get a smoke. Jax leans down, kisses Shanna's forehead, and walks outside.

Shanna sinks in her chair and says, "Yep, totally should have worn a pad."

Shanna walked to the back and grabbed a cig from her pack and headed outside.

The Bacon of Clothing

Date: January 14, 2013

Place: Coyote Creek Trail

Time: 11:30 a.m.

Exactly one year to the date, Jax's divorce became finalized. His annual bike ride up and back down the Coyote Creek Trail is finished. Two hours, eleven minutes is a new record for him.

Jax is taking his cool down very slow as he is sweating profusely and doesn't want to cramp. He is taking laps around his brand new 2013 Chevy Silverado 4x4 black-on-black true dual exhaust with dual flowmasters and eight inch stainless steel tips pointing out the back.

Jax almost loves his truck just as much as his kids. He grabs his water off his bike and tosses his bike up into the bed. He jumps up effortlessly into the bed of the truck and locks it up with a chain to his toolbox.

While Jax is locking his bike up he hears a gentle angelic voice say, "Excuse me!" Jax quickly turns around to see the most beautiful woman he has ever seen. He gets down off his truck and replies, "Hi."

Jax reaches out his hand; the woman extends hers. "I'm Alexis."

"Jax." They shake hands.

"This may sound odd, but I've locked my keys in my car. Would you know a way to get them out?" Alexis knees touch and her hands fidget as if she is asking for some money from her dad, knowing that with that "puppy dog" look, he will say "yes."

"It just so happens I do," he responds. "What car is yours?" Jax inquires.

Alexis smiles with delight and points to a blue Chevy Impala. "Nice," he thought to himself. He motions her to follow him. "Hop in the truck. It's hot, and I'll call my boy for help."

"Okay, as long as you're not going to kidnap me." She laughs nervously.

"No, I was hoping to maybe feed you?" Jax walks around the truck and opens the door for her.

"Wow, and a gentleman." They both smile at each other as she hops in, and Jax shuts the door.

Jax walks in front of the truck, lights a smoke, and opens the door. He places his key in the ignition and turns the power on and starts the truck. Jax turns on the AC and hits his dial button on his steering wheel.

"Call Dusty." Ringing sound comes from the speakers.

"Jax, my brother from another motha."

"Dusty, my brotha, I need your help,"

"Anything for you, Jax."

"I'll shoot you my location on Google maps. A friend of mine locked her keys in her car," states Jax.

"I'll be free at 6:00, and I got you then, brotha," Dusty replies.

"You're the man, Dusty."

"See you soon, J."

Jax flips his cigarette butt out and turns to Alexis. "Looks like you're stuck with me for lunch and possibly dinner."

She just smiles and blushes. "I don't mind at all," she says.

"So I'm dirty and need a shower. Do you mind if we hit my house so I can freshen up?"

"Not at all." She smiles like a school girl in love.

Jax buckles up, and they head out and back to Campbell. Twenty minutes later, they arrive at Jax's house. Jax pulls in the driveway.

"I have to make a call, and I'll come in after," she says.

"Sounds good. Just make yourself at home."

Jax takes his keys out and goes inside. Alexis pulls at her phone and calls her friend Sophia.

"Hey, girl, it worked. I'll be busy the rest of today. I'll call you in the morning." She hangs up fast and heads inside.

Jax stands in front of his shower waiting for the water to warm up, and he calls William.

"Yo," Jax says in an excited tone

"'sup, fool," William replies.

"I met a girl." Jax laughs. "I'll call you in the morning. She seems legit."

"Nice," states William.

"Later." Jax hangs up.

Jax hops in the shower and rinses off and takes the fastest shower ever.

In the meantime Alexis wander around the house and sees the kids' rooms and the baby's room. Luckily, Jax still has his divorce decree still framed in the hallways as a joke. She laughs slightly. She notices Jax's door open and is able to peek in and see Jax in the shower drying off. She is taken back by his physique and blushes and walks back out to the kitchen.

Roughly ten minutes later, Jax reappears.

"I hope you don't mind, I stole a bottle of water," she says.

"Perfectly fine." Jax smiles.

"Okay, let's go," he says as he places his hand on her lower back. Jax isn't much of a talker, but he is feeling the need to open up.

He is kind of shy, but he does feel more relaxed with Alexis. He is normally standoffish but not with her. Jax can't believe a girl like this stumbled into his life. Little does he know that "stumbled" was more like setup.

Little to Jax's knowledge, Alexis was given advice by her best friend Sophia to stage her car keys being locked in her car in order to play "Damsel in Distress." Jax fell for it hook, line, and sinker.

A whirlwind night caught both of them off guard. Alexis really likes Jax. She knows she found a good guy.

Jax has scored a beautiful woman. Too bad she set him up to meet her. But Jax will never know.

After dinner, Jax calls Dusty and has him open up the car and has it driven over to his house since neither of them can drive after so much wine.

Jax spoiled her on the first date. He took her to lunch, then a walk on the beach, played some games, and won her a large teddy bear. He took her to dinner and coffee afterward, where she was introduced to his best friend, Shanna.

Alexis saw how Shanna looked at him and knew she'd have to stay perfect for him to be able to compete with her.

Alexis's car arrives, and Jax collects her keys from Dusty. Jax walks back in and hands Alexis her keys, and Jax sits down on the couch next to her.

Jax offers to open another bottle of wine, but Alexis declines. She says, "I want to remember tonight."

Jax looks up at her, "Oh really? Which part?" he replies.

Alexis leans in and grabs the back of his neck, gently running her finger through his soft brown hair and pulls his mouth to hers and whispers into his ear "This next part," she replies as they kiss.

Jax moves in closer and runs his hand up from her knee to her waist. Jax touches his lips to hers and slides his tongue into her mouth. She reciprocates by sliding her tongue into his and puts her hands up Jax's shirt so she can feel every muscle.

While still attached at the lips, Jax pulls in Alexis close and stands up and slides both hands under her and lifts. She wraps her legs around his hips, and he carries her to the bedroom.

Jax lowers her onto the edge of the bed and removes her blouse. He continues to kiss her and leans her back onto the bed. Jax kisses her neck softly, teasing her collar bone, moving slowly south to kiss and lick both nipples. He slides off her yoga pants and goes in to lick and suck on her sweet spot. After she has a release, Jax slides off his shorts and plunges himself deep inside Alexis. They made love that night and were attached to each other the last four years.

For the first time since his divorce Jax felt whole again.

That next morning Jax woke up, and there lay Alexis. He rolls over and kisses her and wakes her up. Jax and Alexis head into the kitchen, and he makes them breakfast.

Alexis gets dressed and kisses Jax bye. "See you tonight?" she asks.

"You know where I live. Come by," he replies in a joking manner. Jax just stares at Alexis as she walks to her car. He never liked yoga pants but now understands why they are the bacon of clothing.

Four years later, she rarely spends the night. She now fakes and bakes, bleaches her hair platinum blonde, and disappears for days without a call.

And as for today, she will arrive at the inopportune time just to yell at Jax. One question remains: why are her clothes inside out after "yoga class?"

The Crash and Burn

Jax stands outside waiting for Shanna to join him for a cigarette when out of the blue a loud smash and explosion comes from behind him. He ducks and hits the deck. He looks around behind him and sees two vehicles intertwined together. Shanna comes running out, and Jax yells to her to call 911 as he sprints to the white van.

The driver of the white van lays half on her dash and half on her hood, and after that Jax is afraid to see the carnage inside the vehicle. He looks in the back and sees two young children, both crying hysterically, one in a car seat and the other in a booster seat. Jax's heart starts to race as the van is filling up with smoke. He can't open the sliding door. The kids seem to be too young to know how to unlock the doors.

Things seems to become more drastic as they become unconscious. Jax thinks quickly and rips off his shirt, wraps it around his fist, and punches the driver's window open. He unlocks the door and is able to open the sliding door. He undoes the child in the car seat, gets the little girl from the booster seat, and runs the children to Shanna on the curb. Jax looks at the children and says, "Stay here. I have to get your mommy." Jax sees the driver of the little red truck out and safe. He runs over to the white van and turns the lady over. She has her eyes open and is awake. "Help me," she mutters. Jax knows she is fatally injured. When she spoke blood spewed from her mouth and the wound on her chest. Her tongue is punctured and filling with blood fast.

Jax picks her up and turns around. The van, which had been smoking, takes a bad turn for the worse and has a small explosion, which forces Jax and the lady to the ground. Shanna yells for Jax in a panic. Jax replies, "I'm okay; stay back!" Jax has just entered a flashback due to the explosion. It's now 2008, and he's back in Afghanistan. An IED just took out one of the Humvees, and they are taking fire from the north. One of Jax's men, Lance Corporal Coleman, has been fatally wounded, and Jax pulls him out of the Humvee.

The lady coughs up blood as Jax holds her.

"You'll be okay, Coleman," Jax says. The lady's eyes roll back.

"Coleman!" Jax yells.

"Come on, Coleman!" he yells again. Jax, now covered in blood, sees Coleman dead in his arms again.

"Fuck! Coleman! Come back!" he yells as tears flow down his cheeks as he shakes.

Shanna ran over and saw the lady dead in his arms. She walked over and told Jax she was gone and to put her down. Jax doesn't realize it's Shanna. Jax keeps repeatedly asking Shanna for a corpsman. At this point Shanna realized Jax has gone into a flashback. She kneels down next to him, and Shanna looks him in the eyes.

"Jax, come back to me. You're not deployed; you're in Campbell. She's dead; let her go."

Jax looks at Shanna and slowly realizes he's home but not completely. He's stuck in the fog of what's real and what's hallucinations. He looks like a deer caught in headlights. He gently takes his shirt and covers the lady and puts her down. He walks away sore from the blast and covered in blood.

Shanna starts to cry and trails behind Jax as he walks away. The driver of the truck walks up to Jax and asks if he's okay. Jax stops dead in his tracks, looks the man dead in the eyes, reaches back, and punches him square in the face, laying the drunk driver out on the ground. Jax sits on the curb and lights up a cigarette.

Still crying, Shanna walks up slowly. "Jax, are you back?" she asks calmly.

"Yeah. Call Will and tell him to get the kids, please. I'm gonna sit here and work out what happened." Jax's tears are flowing nonstop.

Shanna bends down and hugs him tightly, "It will be okay. You'll be okay." Jax nods, and Shanna heads inside to call Will.

Appearing out of nowhere and from her so-called "yoga class," Alexis walks up behind Jax.

"Jax, where is your shirt? And why is it every time I show up Shanna is hugging you?" Alexis is standing there with her clothes inside out with her hands on her hips.

In a mellow tone Jax answers, "A woman just died in my arms, I almost got blown up, I saved her kids, I punched out the drunk who killed her, I'm covered in blood, and all you care about is my shirt and who's hugging me?" Jax laughs and stands up. He turns and faces Alexis. He stood there and just looked at her. Her face was permanently stuck in resting bitch mode.

"Honey, where is the house key?"

Alexis waves her key chain that's in her hand wrapped around her finger.

"Can I see it?"

Alexis wearily hands over the keys, and Jax takes them from her. As he starts to pull the house key off the keyring, he said, "We are through, by the way. Your clothes are inside out. Sex is a lot different than yoga." He takes his house keys, drops the rest of the keys on the ground, and walks away as she stands there mouth gaping.

Shanna watches as Jax crosses the street away from Alexis. As Jax crosses the street, he looks left and sees the dead woman again. As soon as he reaches the curb, Jax looks down and sees Coleman again at his feet. Jax hits his knees and grabs Coleman.

"I got you, Nick; you're okay." Jax starts crying again.

"Don't let me die, Staff," Coleman stammers.

"I got you, Nicky, I got you!"

Shanna calls William to hurry up. She has been watching all of this and knows it can get dangerous really fast. Coleman takes his last breath, "No, Nick, no, no, no, no. Please!" Jax slams both his hands on the ground.

"*No*!"

Shanna comes outside, "Jax, please come in." Jax looks up and sees Shanna; he looks back down, and Coleman is gone. All he can do is cry. Jax stands up and walks to Shanna and grabs her and cries into her shoulder with an embrace that screams he needs her. She rubs his back and strokes his hair, telling him that everything will be okay. Shanna walks him to the back and gives him a towel and a T-shirt from the coffee shop. She shows Jax into the bathroom and lets him wash up.

The Kids

Jax stands in Shanna's bathroom, cleaning off, when his kids arrive. All of them pour into her office and see their dad covered in blood.

"Dad, are you okay?" His oldest daughter asks.

"It's not your Dad's blood, hon." Shanna explains.

"Ohhh. Okay. What can we eat, Dad?"

"Whatever you want, Kaylie. All of you go pick out a sandwich and drink." Jax explains. He looks down at his leg and sees his five year old isn't moving after gripping tightly to his leg.

"Hi, Bubba, I missed you, too." His son kisses his leg and runs off.

"Will," he says.

"I'm on it, Jax."

Jax looks at Shanna, and she sighs and smiles at him. Jax finishes washing up and puts on his shirt.

"You sure you two can swing this with the kids?" Jax walks up to Shanna one pace away.

"Yes, I'm sure J. We've got this." Shanna rubs both his arms and pulls him in for a hug. Jax reaches up and moves Shanna's hair from her face and places each hand lightly on her cheeks.

Jax moves in and both of their eyes close as their lips touch. They each feel as if time stopped and they are floating. Their lips are locked as their tongues collide into one another—a moment nine years in the making.

Shanna's body falls into Jax's as their kiss seems like it won't end. Shanna moans, and it sends chills down Jax's spine. This arouses Jax, and he presses it up against Shanna, which causes an even bigger moan. Jax bites down on Shanna's bottom lip as he pulls away, worried one of the kids will see.

A knock at the door sends them shooting five feet in opposite directions. William comes walking in.

"Jen is on her way to get the kids, Bro. I'll take you to the VA after."

"Tracking," Jax acknowledges.

"'bout time, you two. Jax, lose the boner," William points out smirking.

"Shut it, asshole. Bye," Jax says as he slams the door, "I'm gonna spend a few with the kids, okay?"

Shanna nods as she is still fifty shades of red.

Jax walks out of the office and steps out to the corner and sees the kids. Kaylin 17, Parker 15, Ava 10, and Lucas 5, are playing with their uncle William and eating their bear claws. Jax sees his whole world in front of him and knows he needs to get help now, so he can be there for them.

It's just not all about him anymore. After thirty seconds, he emerges and makes himself known.

"So track me, kiddos. Daddy has to go to the VA for a little bit, and I will be back soon, okay?" All of them mutter "Tracking, Dad."

"Why?" Kylie asks.

"I have a head issue, and I need fixing." Jax answered.

"Why?" She asks again.

"Combat, Kaykay. Just leave it at that 'til you're older,"

"Okay, Dad."

Jax spends a minute with each kid, telling each one he loves them, and they can visit later if they want.

Jen arrives and hugs Jax and reassures him she will work with Shanna and William while she is at work and has her weekends off.

They all hug and kiss one last time and head out the door.

Jax walks to the office and shuts the door behind him. Shanna is sitting at her desk. She takes off her glasses and stands and walks to the center of the room.

"Hey," she states

"Hey," he answers.

They both laugh as they both reached out and grabbed each other's hands.

"So I broke up with Alexis earlier when she showed up." He smiles, "I was planning that kiss a few days from now, so that happened early. They both laughed a bit.

"I guess a real date after this gets worked out?"

"You better, Marine!"

Jax leans in and a tango breaks out between their lips. Jax pulls her in tight and wraps both arms around her like it was the final goodbye between them. Jax releases her. "Come see me?"

"Anything for you, Marine"

"Awesome, Banana."

Jax slowly walks away and leaves the office.

"Def gonna need batteries and wine tonight!"

The Ride

Jax and William sit in William's truck on the way to the VA. Jax is in the passenger seat and lights up a cigarette. "I don't know how I am going to do this, Will," Jax says in a sad tone, "I never thought I'd get this weak."

William interrupts, "First off, J., don't even think that shit. Second, you're not weak," William demands. He continues, "Many of our brothers and sisters got weak and didn't get help, God rest their souls, but suicide is the weak way out. Being strong is facing the PTSD and saying "Fuck *you*!" You're the strongest man I know, bravest I've ever served with, def more man than me." William says proudly.

"What are you saying, Will?" Jax asks.

"Remember a few years ago I got 'sick' while in New York?"

"Yeah, why?"

William continues, "I wasn't sick. I had a mental breakdown, and my PTSD was out of control. I was on a twenty-one-day psych hold." Will explains.

Jax turns in his seat and faces Will. "So that's why you disappeared?"

"Yes."

"I didn't know how, plus I know you battle the same shit, so why add to your misery."

"I'm sorry, Will. You can tell me anything; you should know that."

"Okay, bro, thanks"

"Still doesn't explain why didn't you tell me?"

"Just didn't seem relevant. You are and always have been the strong one in the unit. You never showed signs that our deployments affected you this way."

"I've always had to be the strong one for the kids, but now I have no control over what's going on." Jax tears up.

"Jax you have an amazing family and kids who love you dearly. You have a new girl who loves you more than you know, and she has been there for you for, what? Like ten years? Shit, man. You got hundreds of friends who got your back. We will all work with Jen to make sure the kids are taken care of."

"If you're in charge of the kids, who is in charge of you?" Jax and Will laugh.

"Look, Bro, it won't be overnight, but it is better than a barrel in your mouth. And please follow the process. Don't put up that wall and shut down. I know you."

"What wall?" Jax asks, looking at William puzzled and guilty.

"You know damn well what wall!"

"I need that wall, bro."

"No, you don't; you're not a kid anymore."

"Okay." Jax looks into his lap.

Jax and William pull up to the drop off area in front of the ER. They sat in silence staring into the hospital, not wanting to say good bye.

"Jax . . ."

Jax interrupts

"Shut up, fag. I'll call you later."

Jax smiles and hits Will in the shoulder.

"Tracking," Will responds.

Jax exits the truck and walks away.

The VA Hospital

Seventy-five and sunny, not a cloud in the sky. Jax sits sloppily in a chair as he waits for others to arrive. He notices how plain the room is. It's like they want no distractions while you're in group. Twenty or so chairs in a circle formation in a plain egg-shell-colored room.

A young man walks in, five-eight, average build, brown hair, and light eyes. He is sporting the high and tight with a beard. The young man speaks up, "Is this the PTSD circle group?"

Jax looks around, "What gives it away? The chairs in a circle?" Jax laughs.

The man replies "Who pissed in your cheerios?"

Jax looks him up and down, "You a Marine?" Jay asks.

"What gave it away?" The young man takes a seat across from Jax.

"0311" he says.

"Same here" replies Jax.

Both of them stand up and shake hands. They pick out two chairs away from the door, sit next to each other, and start to exchange banter.

Jax asked, "You OIF (Operation Iraqi Freedom)?"

"Yeah, you?"

"Yeah."

"Cool. Checks out. I'm Nick. So, you see and hear shit, too?"

"Jax. Both."

"Checks out."

Jax asked, "Rank?"

"E-3, you?"

"E-6." Jax laughs.

Nick exclaimed, "Fuck you!"

Jax answered, "Don't hate 'cause I outrank you on top of being better looking."

"Whatever, staph infection" Nick makes the hashtag sign with his hands. "Hashtag Dick Bag."

"Hashtag, suck my dick in this box." Both laugh. "Best skits Justin Timberlake and Fallon did by far."

Nick said, "Fuck ya. I'm Justin, though."

Jax disagreed, "Hell no! I'm JT. I outrank you, plus your voice is too nasally to be Justin."

Nick told him, "Fuck this group shit; I'm out of here. Later, Staff hashtag. Bye-bye."

"You fucker."

Jax sits there as Nick leaves just in time as the doctor walks in. Now Jax is stuck and can't leave the group.

After two hours of being trapped in the group, Jax struggles to find Nick. So after a few minutes he gives up and heads to the smoking section located in a closed-off, nonescapable area in the furthest corner.

Jax opens the door, and to his surprise, Nick is out there smoking already. "Perfect timing."

Nick laughs, "How was group?"

"I see why you left."

"All groups do is make me want to drink."

Both laugh. Jax pulls out a cigarette and lights it, saying, "Ya, checks out. How long have you been here?"

"A while. Hopefully I'll go home soon.

Jax asked, "Where you from?"

"New Jersey"

"What the fuck you doing out here?"

"Long story, not enough time."

"Aw, one of those."

"You?"

"Couple of days. I live thirty minutes away in Campbell."

"How did you break?"

Jax explained, "Started with a bad dream as usual and went downhill from there. Saw a car wreck, pulled a lady out, and snapped after that."

"Damn, Bro, that's tough."

"Yeah." Jax pulls in a drag and inhales.

"So what do you see?" "An old friend."

"Who was it?"

"A guy from my unit. It's not important. Why you pushing?" Jax gets annoyed a little.

"'Cause it is important."

"No, it's not, Bro; just let it go!" Jax puts out his cigarette and starts to walk away.

Nick says one last thing. "It's important to me, Staff Sergeant. You are the one who let me die.

Jax stops, turns around, and slowly walks forward, inspecting Nick from head to toe. "It can't be you. I held you when you died. I buried you myself."

Jax scrambles to light another cigarette.

"It's me, Staff."

"No, you're not real."

Jax struggles to light his cigarette; his eyes fill with tears.

"Then why am I here? I'm here 'cause of you. You didn't kill me, but you blame yourself for my death."

"You're not real, Nick."

"I'm real because you make me real."

"I had to hold your wife together and comfort her. I've raised Ava as my own when Susie killed herself. I've done everything to make up for your death."

Jax gets right in front of Nick. "I didn't kill you. You were on the Humvee behind me. That IED took everyone out. When I pulled you out, the corpsman tried to get the shrapnel out of your neck but couldn't. You wanted me to pull it, but I couldn't. I was stuck."

Jax falls to his knees. Two of Jax's doctors watch all of this from inside the building and continue to look on.

Jax is crying like he lost Coleman all over again. "I'm sorry I failed you then, and I'm sorry I failed you now." Jax looks up at Nick.

"That's what you don't get, Jax. I wasn't you. We were at war. It's what happens. People die. My number was up, Staff Sergeant."

Jax looks back down. "Your daughter talks about you a lot."

"I'll always be around her because of you."

Jax looks up, and Nick is gone. Jax stumbles getting up and calls out for Nick to come back.

The doctors come out.

Dr. Mendoza asks, "You okay, Mr. Guerra?"

"No, not even close."

"Please come in and talk with us."

"Okay, Doc."

The Team

The doctors stand there with the doors open as they usher Jax in. Jax staggers past them into the hallway. The older of the doctors motions to follow them, and so Jax does, from one hallway to the next hallway. He follows them and arrives at a room close to the group meeting room.

Bright baby blue walls pop out at Jax first, then a wall full of certificates and degrees from San Jose State, Stanford, and Oxford. Obviously he is a well-accomplished doctor. The oldest doctor takes a seat behind the classic three-sided desk, and the other doctors follow them inside and sit along the wall.

Jax takes a seat in front of the desk and stares into his lap. He notices his hands are shaking and places them under his legs.

"Jax, we are your team of doctors. I'm Doctor Robertson, the lead resident." The doctor points to the first doctor, a middle-aged man with salt-and-pepper hair, roughly 200 pounds of slob, but at least he has a nice smile and gentle blue eyes. "This is Doctor Mendoza, your group psychologist, who you met earlier today. The doctor says "Hello," and Doc Robertson points to the left and signals to the final doctor.

"Jax, you following us so far?"

Jax nods but could not care less at this point. All he wants is a razor blade to cut himself to make the pain go away.

"This is Doctor Eve Lassen, your one-on-one psychologist and therapist.

Jax looks up and cracks a smile out of habit and acknowledged her. She is a very young, tall, slender doctor fresh out of school. Very beautiful to say the least. She gives off the naughty teacher vibe with her hair in a bun and glasses that magnify her emerald green eyes.

"Jax, can you tell us what we just saw outside on the smoking deck?"

Jax looks up from his lap, tears freely streaming down his face and neck being soaked up by his V-neck shirt. He tries to speak up but can't create the sounds he needs. He feels like yelling, "Fuck you!" but simply lowers his head and covers his face with his hands.

Jax's imagination sparks up memories of him as a young boy in his room at a foster home, cutting himself with little cuts on his chest, leaving long trails of blood, making his world pain go away by inflicting physical pain. The sight of blood gave him pleasure as it dripped down his body. Jax is fully down the rabbit hole and doesn't see a way out.

Jax is lost and doesn't understand anything that's going on. His sight and what's he is hearing has hit a whole new level of fucked. What once was in his head is now out in the world. He feels weak and doesn't know how he has been strong all these years. But what he hasn't learned yet is PTSD preys on you, no matter who you are. It doesn't matter whether you are weak or strong, black or white. If PTSD wants you, it will take you down. PTSD isn't racist or sexist. PTSD is a predator with a great infiltration skill, better than any soldier or Marine could be. Dr. Robertson asks "Jax, are you having auditory and or visual hallucinations or both?"

Jax nods.

"Wow, both. I'm sorry for that. We will start you on some meds to help with those. It may take a while to feel the full effects of them, so we will supplement with Adavan to start, which will help with anxiety."

Jax nods again and stands up. "May I lie down?"

"Yes, you may. A nurse will be in to see you with some meds in a few, Jax. Okay?"

"Yes, sir."

Jax turns and leaves the office.

Doctor Robertson stands up and says, "Watch him very closely, team. Marines like him can be violent without notice and a loose cannon when a strong flashback occurs."

Both doctors nod at Doctor Lassen's inputs.

"He does seem perceptive enough to want treatment, so we have a good chance to help him."

"You're correct, Doctor. I'm thinking 52/50 hold for forty-five days."

Doctor Lassen and Doctor Mendoza both nod and concur with Dr. Robertson.

The Final Crack

Jax walks slowly and weakened with a solemn look on his face tattooed with tears. He struggles to walk straight, but his legs are shaking and weak. After turning down his hallway, rifles sound off, and mortar explosions hit next to him. Jax jumps and sprawls out on the floor. He looks up and sees the young boy with a knife in his chest walk into his room. Jax covers his ears as women's screams echo through the hallway.

A nurse quickly rushes around the corner as she was startled by Jax's screams and sobbing. She slides in and wraps her arms around Jax.

Nurse Mariah was a corpsman for twenty years and lost her husband of thirty years to PTSD, so she has a huge heart for marines but even more so for people who suffer from PTSD.

"You'll be okay, Mr. Guerra," she reassures him.

Jax is on his knees and leans into Nurse Mariah. Crying and covering his ears. Bullets are blazing and bombs echoing as if he is back in Afghanistan.

Two male nurses arrive and take Jax up by his arms and help him to his feet. He can barely stand. They get Jax into bed and struggle to sedate him.

They are able to secure his arms and legs in wraps that tie to the bed. They inject a sedative cocktail into Jax's hip.

"This is for your protection, Jax," Nurse Mariah explains.

Jax yells profanities and struggles to get loose. He fails.

Nurse Mariah stays with Jax until the meds kick in, and he passes out. She remains, holding his hand.

Santos

For the first time in years, Jax has slept all night. But leave it to the Marine Corps–issued internal clock to wake him up at 0600. For the first time in years, Jax doesn't wake up sweaty and sticking to the sheets. Jax goes back to sleep for a couple more hours.

After a brief nap, Jax wakes up, and he is no longer shackled to his bed. He pops up in a cheerful fashion and hits the deck and does his morning pushups. After one set, a nurse comes in and is surprised to see Jax on the floor.

"Mr. Guerra, if you could stop soldiering for a moment, I'd like to give you your pills for this morning and take you to chow."

Jax stood there shocked, mouth open. He looks at the nurse as if she was speaking Spanish or German.

"Ma'am, I do *not* soldier. I am a Marine, an elite fighting machine. Soldiers are in the Army or Girl Scouts."

Jax, very pleased with himself, stands there smiling with a half-cocked smile, arms folded. Nurse Cain steps forward.

"Mr. Guerra, I don't care what you *were*. Right now you're my patient who needs to take pills and eat chow."

"Yes, ma'am," he responds in a respectful fashion and follows the portly old nurse as he puts on his shirt.

Jax arrives at the chow hall and takes his seat. To his surprise, there are a lot of patients, male and female, all veterans. His first and only thought was, *I guess I'm not alone*.

Nurse Cain walks up and places a small cup of pills in front of Jax and slams his plate of eggs, hash browns, and toast in front of him.

"Take these pills and show me your mouth after, please, Mr. Guerra."

Jax pops the pills, drinks some water, and sticks his tongue out at the nurse, then opens wide.

Nurse Cain, who is now nicknamed in Jax's head as Nurse Ratchette, just rolls her eyes and walks out of the chow hall.

Jax stares down at his plate and sighs. Tapping his fork on the plate caught the ear of an older vet at the table in front of him. Jax is in a daydream of Shanna, remembering her kiss and how her hands felt on his body. How he ran his hands through her hair, and his hands didn't even get caught. How her body felt colliding with his and feeling her breathe heavier as they were chest to chest.

Bang! A plate crashes on the table.

The old vet stands there, smiling with a huge shit-eating grin, totally happy with himself for startling the youngster.

"Santos, Sgt Santos Figueroa, 101st Airborne Screaming Eagles Paratroopers, Vietnam. Rumor is you're a fucking leatherneck OIF.

Jax looks at the man and takes a bite of eggs and chews.

"So you're loud when orgasming and a Girl Scout trooper? Nice!"

"Oh a smartass, are we?"

"A bit."

"Then we will get along just fine, jarhead."

"So you sure know a lot there, Sarge."

"My room is next to where the docs meet."

"Must be nice, I guess."

"How long did you serve, youngster?"

"Eight years, you?"

"Six."

Santos stands up and reaches out his hand. Shaky, but Jax obliged the gesture. "Take care, Jarhead. I'll see you in group. Have to piss; it's hell getting old."

"Checks out."

Santos leaves in a rush. Jax can hear him making his way to the bathroom as he hears faint shouting to get out of his way.

The First Visit

Jax sits looking at his empty plate, wondering about his kids. What are they doing? Are they okay? Do they have any boo-boos? It also crossed his mind whether he brought his trash cans in from the curb. He thought about William and his dumb ass. He thought about God and how he can find his way back to Him. But primarily, he thought about Shanna. He thinks back to the kiss and how this hospital visit will affect their relationship, or if they will even have one. He has been labeled as crazy now, so who would want a crazy guy as a husband or boyfriend? Question after question passes through his mind. Doubt after doubt pass through as well, destroying the short-term happiness he creates. After an hour of self-pity and doubt he flusters himself into a smoke break.

Jax grabs his empty cup and plate and places them with all the others and stands there staring. The only question on his mind is, "What the hell am I doing here, God?" He hangs his head and exits the mess hall.

Walking out, he makes a left and heads back to the smoking area. With an over-irritated tone of voice, Nurse Cain calls for Jax. "SSgt Guerra! You have a visitor."

Jax stops dead in his tracks and heads back to the front desk. She walks away with rude swagger as if she were the boss. Jax looks over to the desk and there she was.

He couldn't help but stop and just stand there. She stood there looking the other way, not having noticed Jax yet, which gave him more time to just stand there and stare. She was perfect. She was the key, and that scared the hell out of him. He knew she wasn't perfect, but all her good and bad and flaws and strengths made her perfect just for him, from the red hair down to her cute little toes.

Her bright red hair flowed around her like an angel's halo. Her skin is kissed by flawless sunshine, and her soul brightens this cloudy day. Her cotton dress hugs her body as if magnetized to her. She sees Jax, and he smiles at her. She starts to turn red, and the tears start to flow. She walks to him with her arms out, crying. As they meet, the world stops for Jax. For Shanna, she now knows he is safe and secure and feels relief. Jax feels calm and home; he feels a sense of purpose as a man. There is something that boosts a man when he is loved by a woman. He becomes untouchable and can accomplish anything.

With a broken and choked-up voice, Jax offers to go outside to the smoking area. Still choked up, he grabs her again and gives her a huge hug and spins around and cries more. He puts her down and kisses her as if it was his last chance to do so. The passion that ignited with that kiss made Shakespeare jealous and cupid turn red.

"Sorry." They hug tighter.

Shanna says, "Don't be, baby. We all love you; you did nothing wrong. I love you, you jackass." She bumps his shoulder as they head to the patio to smoke and talk.

Jax responded, "I love you, too. But you all have to realize this burden is mine and mine alone. I don't want to impede on your life or Will's like this.

Shanna grabs his face and gets real close. "You listen to me, Mr. Marine Bad Ass. You're mine, and that means all of you, not just the good days, love. But the bad days too and the so-so days. That's how much I love you and how much the kids love you, and of course there is love somewhere in there for William. Plus, have you seen me on my period? Come on. I'm crazy one week a month. I can deal with you, Jax. We are a team. From good to bad to crazy to making love to fighting to tickle fights to you not putting the seat down, I'm all in with you, Jax."

Shanna looks at Jax who is just stuck and looks like a deer caught in headlights; he is speechless for the moment. Then Jax laughs and turns more toward Shanna.

"Of course I do, Banana." He shrugs, and she motions like she is going to hit him again.

"You better, damn it. 'Cause as God as my witness, I'll beat you 'til you pray again and get back on the right path. And put a ring on this." Shanna laughs and is joking but kind of isn't. She has been waiting for this moment for years.

As they chat outside, Jax tries to be cool and sneaky. He grabs Shanna and spins her around and kisses her. It would have been great if his lip didn't smash her nose, tongue smashed into her face, and bottom lip in her mouth.

"Jax, what the hell?" Shanna spits and wipes her face off and walks away.

"Well, shit, that was supposed to be some almost cool romantic *Notebook* type shit." He steps toward Shanna, and she lifts her hand really fast and motions him to stop and back off.

Jax asks, "So . . . how are my babies?"

With a glare she looks at Jax as if she was going to whoop his butt. She finishes wiping her face and lights a cigarette. "They are fine. Ava is confused but thinks you see her dad's ghost."

Jax said, "It's going to be rough on them. It may be a while before they let me out of here, Babe. I'm worried shit will hit the fan if I'm in here too long."

Shanna replied, "Don't worry about anything, Jax. We have everything under control. Your emergency go-bag came in handy. We have all the credit cards and the kids' info we will need for the school and everything; it's fine. Jen is working with us, and it's okay."

Shanna places her hand on Jax's leg as they sit there. She moves her hand up slowly to his inner thigh, saying, "I got your front, not just your back, baby."

She throws a wink at him.

"You got it, Banana"

They wrap arms around one another and kiss nice and slow, and once again time stands still as they float through space.

The Group: Day 5

Jax stands in the smoking area, having a midday smoke break, when Santos joins him on the patio and said, "Give me one of the bad boys, jarhead."

Jax steps back and says, "*No way*! Not after your wife almost killed me the last time, you old bastard." They both laugh, and Santos just stands there smelling Jax's second-hand smoke and enjoying every minute of it.

Santos said, "She is here. She is in Modesto, visiting Carmen over off of Coffee with her sister!"

"You said that last time. And halfway through you smoking it and coughing half your lungs up, she showed up and almost throttled me."

"Well, the fudge you, Marine!"

Jax retorts, "Love you, too, Girl Scout!"

Santos walks away and turns back as he opens the door. "By the way, Jax, its group time. I came out to tell you that. You're late." He smiles and walks in for group.

Jax puts out his smoke and walks in right behind Santos.

Santos asked, "You going to actually share today, jarhead?"

Jax makes a funny noise and face as he motions no and laughs, "Hell no!"

Santos slaps Jax on the back. "That's my jarhead!"

They both walk into the room with their arms around each other making tons of noise as they enter, making Dr. Mendoza glare at them and bark at them to sit down and be quiet. They tried to sit together but were quickly separated for the better of the group, which made them only sit exactly across from at each other, making faces and still acting up.

Dr. Mendoza greeted the group: "Welcome, everyone, how is everyone doing today?" He looks around the room, expecting an answer but never once has anyone ever volunteered information to this jerk.

Jax answered, "Oh, just peachy, Doc!" Dr. Mendoza just glares at Jax.

"Why are you peachy, Jax? This should be good."

"Because I am. Drugs."

Dr. Mendoza instructed, "Today I want you to concentrate on your meditation and *tapping* exercises." Jax stands up.

"Jax, where are you going?"

"To go meditate and tap myself 'til I fall asleep." Jax laughs and starts to head out of the room.

Santos, of course, is roaring in laughter. "There's my jarhead!"

Dr. Mendoza warned him, "Don't encourage him, Mr. Figueroa."

Jax walks out of the room. Dr. Mendoza chases Jax and stops him.

"Jax, stop. Why don't you take group seriously?"

"I will when I'm ready."

"Very well."

Jax walks away and goes into his room and lies down.

The Zip Ties: Day 7

Jax sits in a sun-soaked courtyard staring off into oblivion. A tear forms in Jax's eyes. Not wanting to acknowledge the salty water dripping, he doesn't wipe.

Jax is so entrenched with his thoughts, he hasn't realized Dr. Eve Lassen has taken a seat opposite of him and is studying him.

After a few moments Eve makes a sound to clear her throat. Jax looks up and quickly wipes his tear-soaked face. Dr. Lassen opens her notebook and readies her pen.

Jax leans back on the bench, sighs, and crosses his arms. He looks up. "We are going to talk about this, aren't we?"

"Yes, Jax."

Jax lets the tears continue to fall and leans forward with his elbows on his knees. "I am not sure where to start, Doc."

"The beginning is always the best, Jax. Be detailed and tell the story as best you can."

Jax stares at Eve with a look she has never seen on a Marine. Jax has a lost-child look who is stuck like he is in trouble.

"I was eight years old. I was with a new family in San Jose. I was happy because my social worker said the man was a police officer or sheriff. I felt safe once I met him and his wife. She was sweet and very pretty. He was very tall and in good shape. After being in a home where they beat me, this seemed like it could be a forever home.

"The first week was fine. New school, new friends. New mom who was a nurse who she worked nights while he worked days. So it seemed legit to me. He was very stern but also very gentle.

"He was a drinker, so he would pass out by 10:00 and left me alone in my room. The second week was starting to seem odd. He would all of a sudden shower with me and would wash me. I was scared to say anything because he was bigger than me. I kept quiet and let the showers continue into the third and fourth week."

Jax starts shaking and crying harder than he has ever cried. "Jax, take a breath, but keep letting your emotions flow. This is very healthy, and I'm so proud of you. Please continue."

"He had me lie on my stomach and place my hands behind my back and zip-tied my hands. He flipped me over and started playing with my genitals. He squeezed my testicles when I tried to move away.

He then zip-tied my legs at my ankles and spread some kind of lotion on my feet to masturbate. He released and cut me loose and left. That treatment lasted a couple weeks."

Jax stops and covers his face and starts to sob. Dr. Lassen places her hand on Jax's back to comfort him.

Jax wipes his face and continues.

"He got bored with the same thing after a couple weeks, and one night he bent me over and started to sexually assault me anally. Every few thrusts he would hit me and knock the wind out of me. After a few weeks of this, my anger grew and grew. One night we watched a scary movie, and I got ideas about how to stop this. I waited until he passed out one night, and I opened the front door, I went into his room, and I plunged a steak knife into his groin. He jumped out of bed.

"He hit the floor, and I was out the door and ran to an open garage where some guys were drinking. I asked them to call 911. I was taken to the hospital and given a rape kit and blood workups and they pulled DNA out of me."

"Jax, I don't know what the fuck to say to you. I've never in my career heard a story so haunting."

"This was the first of six men who would sexually molest me. Thirty-two homes beat me. Out of the forty, seven sexually abused me. One was amazing.

"I'm so proud of you, Jax, but I'm going to have to ask Dr. Robertson how to address this."

"That's fine."

Dr. Lassen gets up and walks away. She enters the building and goes around the corner. She puts her back against the wall and breaks down crying.

The Marine I Once Was: Day 10

Jax slowly walks into the group room, knowing he was going to get "the look" from Dr. Mendoza since he was late. His anxiety soared, also knowing whoever is latest had to share. He hesitated as he hit the door threshold. "Well, Jax, looks like the hot seat is yours today."

Jax nervously cracks a shit-eating grin and takes a seat. He rubs his hands over his knees and wipes the sweat pouring out of his hands.

"Jax, today we are discussing our PTSD, and what's our earliest memory that triggers it. What is the memory that is your primary trigger for your PTSD episodes?"

Jax sighs and doesn't want to speak but knows exactly what the doc is asking."

"Can't we do this in private, Doc?"

"No."

"Fuck. It's the killing. It's seeing my brothers being KIA. It, the blood, the guts, broken bodies, the torn-apart bodies. It's being away from the kids, the wives. Not feeling like America is home anymore."

Jax pauses as he zones out. Jax has mentally been transported back to Iraq. He sees and smells and feels like he is back in the sandbox of hell. He's looking down and describes it.

"It's blood-soaked clothes and boots. The sand beneath my feet and not like sand at the beach but a hard grainy dirt that feels like cement when you fall on it. It's my unit surrounding me in our tent as we mourn the loss of Master Gunnery Sgt Davis. It's holding his dog tags and not wanting to let go. It's the blood getting sticky as it curdles in your hands. It's wanting to die because you lost a brother."

Jax wipes his eyes and shrugs to what the doctor is saying. Jax is having another big breakthrough as he learns how to deal with his past that haunts him.

"Group, thank you for your participation. This will wrap up this morning's group, and I will see you for check-in later.

Everybody claps and files out of the room. All except Jax. He sits there alone for the next hour, thinking over what he had said. He doesn't like being vulnerable, yet feels it is spiritually lifting.

Jax starts thinking about Shanna and what she is doing. The distance between them is small but being locked down makes it feel as if she's a million miles away.

Soon enough she will be back in his arms and happy once again—she will be visiting again this weekend.

Sobriety and Jesus: Day 12

Jax sits in the lobby staring out at the nothing zone. The nothing zone is a space Jax loves to go into, it's a mentally built fortress of solitude where he sits in nothingness and lets life pass by. It is where he can sit in peace and quiet and nothing bothers him. They only last a few moments, but he loves the brief solitude. Dr. Mendoza had said something that didn't necessarily upset him or bother him, but it tweaked him about his past still following him after all these years.

"Why does it have to play a part in my life today? I have been sober for years. I did it to myself, he thought. It is just hard to have that keep popping up after all these years." Jax sits and remembers all the times he had while drinking and on drugs. Everyone always says weed was the gateway drug but it's the best medicine Jax has. But it was the ecstasy and the cocaine that really had his back to the wall. There wasn't a day that went by in those five years where he didn't spend it swimming at the bottom of a bottle.

Then came the cocaine, then the shroom and pills. "The pain pills were bad days," he thought and laughed to himself. He never got into heroin or anything else other than that, which is intense and stupid to say the least. But after a five-year run of booze, drugs, and women, he has his epiphany moment where he found himself face-to-face with his Maker.

His adoptive mother had just passed, and he took a whole bottle of Vicodin and whole bottle of whiskey and tried to kill himself. Needless to say, he failed. The only thing that saved him was being in that church parking lot when he did it. The pastor found him and got him help. His wife at the time left him afterward, taking the kids.

Jax went six months in a rehab step-down program, and he has been sober since. But that isn't the important part to the story that Jax likes to tell. His face starts to crack a smile, for in his head he is now thinking of when he flatlined and saw Jesus. Or so he thinks, but he believes the voice he talked to was Jesus.

Jax zones out again, but this time it's a deep zone where the world has gone and is in a full daydream. He walks up to this light, and a voice booms from it.

"Jax, You do not belong here, you foolish boy." Jax stumbles backwards a few steps, butt hanging out of his hospital gown and all.

He was in awe and speechless when the voice booms again, "Jax, your friends and kids you need you. A selfish road like this only breeds hate with those who you left behind."

He remembers hitting his knees and begging for forgiveness, but the voice never spoke after that. The light got hotter and brighter, and the next thing he knew he woke up three days later in the ICU. He hasn't touched any drugs since and can manage to have a beer or two without getting out of control. Jax stands up and walks to his room. A single tear falls, Jax smiles, thinking to himself, "God is still *good*."

The Family: Day 14

It's Friday at 3:30, and Shanna sits patiently waiting for William to drop off the kids for the weekend. Two of the kids come ripping in. She greets them, "Girls!"

Kaylen asks, "Is Dad here?"

"No, sweetie, he will be back on September 30."

"That's forever."

"I know, honey." Shanna hugs both the girls tight.

Ava asked, "Is Daddy still seeing my dad?

"I don't know, Ava. Your dad is in heaven protecting your mom."

"Okay, Nana."

Shanna wipes a tear from her eyes and asks, "Where are those icky boys?"

Kaylen answered, "Slowly walking."

William and Jax's sons are going at their own pace since Lucas is only five. He goes at his own pace, looking and touching everything. William stands holding the door to the coffee shop, watching Lucas.

William told him, "Lucas, come on, kid."

Lucas looks up and smiles and waddles faster in William's direction until a lady walks by him and says hello to him. He then stopped and started following her. She stops and laughs.

William said, "Lucas, you're just like your dad. Come on. Sorry, ma'am."

She smiles and walks away.

William exclaimed, "You have good taste, kid." He puts up his hands to high-five Lucas. They turn and walk into the coffee shop.

Lucas yells with joy, "Nana!

William puts him down, and he runs to Shanna. He trips and falls and doesn't cry. He looks around and says, "Shit" as he brushes himself off.

Shanna scolds him, "Lucas Alexander! You're just like your daddy."

Shanna picks him up and gives him a raspberry on his belly, which is showing.

Kaylen asks, "Thirty days more without Dad?" She runs into the office. Shanna tries to stop her.

William told Shanna, "Let her go and chill. She is like her mom and needs to cry it out for a bit."

"Poor thing. Okay, kids."

Shanna puts Lucas on a chair and has Parker and Ava sit down.

Shanna asks them, "So what to drink? Hot cocoa? Cider with some egg sandwiches on a croissant?"

All the kids yell, "YEEAAHHHHH"

William says, "I got Kaylen. Make her cocoa and a sandwich."

William loves Kaylen as his own as he is her godfather. William walks to the office in the back of the shop and walks in after knocking on the door.

Kaylen sniffles and says, "Please leave me alone."

William plops down on the couch in Shanna's office right behind Kaylen, sighs, and wraps his arm around Kaylen, and she falls into his chest, crying and covering her face.

"Kay-kay, I've known your dad since 2000, ever since he joined my unit. I've seen him at his best and at his worst as a man and as a Marine." William plays with her hair and continued, "Did you know the happiest I ever seen your dad was the day you were born? Best day of my life, too! I gained a best friend January 26, 2001. Your dad is the strongest man and best man I know. He has been through a lot, and he and I had to do a lot of unthinkable things to people overseas. We both have issues over it."

Kaylen wipes her tears.

"Did Daddy have to kill people?"

"Ycs, sweetie, he did, and some of them are younger than you. So you have to realize he needs us more than ever right now. You're the oldest and need to be strong for your brothers and sister."

"Okay. Especially Ava?"

"Yes, especially Ava!"

Kaylen curls up in William's chest and hugs him. "Thank you, Uncle Will."

William kisses the top of her head and picks her up. "Anytime, my little monkey!"

William carries out Kaylen and starts to tickle her so that everyone hears her infectious laugh. Kaylen is sixteen and Jax's pride and joy. The day she was born changed his life for the better. He walked taller and fought harder. She is 5 feet, 9 inches, blonde, blue eyes, weighs 125 pounds, and looks so small in William's arms. William couldn't be prouder of his goddaughter and protects her as if she is his own, especially when boys come around.

Kaylen runs out of William's arms and hugs Shanna behind the counter and asks, "Need any help, Mamma?"

Shanna, taken aback, chokes back a tear as she replies, "No, sweetie, I got this, but see if your brothers and sister have any homework, please."

"Okay."

Kaylen jumps up, kisses Shanna on the cheek, and goes off to help her siblings. William is still standing there laughing as Shanna tears up.

Shanna told him, "Shut up, Will"

"I guess she's okay with you and Jax. Now all you got to do is get Jax to settle down." Shanna laughs and continues making the kids their drinks and food.

William says, "Going for a smoke."

"Bye! Assbag!"

"Heard that!"

Shanna says, "I know."

The Childhood: Day 21

At the next conference, Dr. Robertson asked, "Jax we have reached day 21. How are you feeling about your meds and the treatment you have received thus far?"

Jax looks over to his left out the window and runs his hands over the arms of the chair. "It's still hard, but I can tell the difference from what's real and what's not. The sounds aren't as loud."

Dr. Robertson spoke to the other doctors. "Team?"

Dr. Mendoza says, "Jax has improved and does participate a little bit in group."

Dr. Lassen added, "Jax and I will meet for another one-on-one today and dive deeper into his youth, rather than combat."

Dr. Robertson says, "Okay, great. Jax, do you have any questions or feelings to share? I will adjust your meds a bit but not much."

"Nope, I'm good."

"Okay. Thank you, Jax and team. We will meet again in about ten days and discuss discharge and continued treatment. That is all."

Jax and the doctors stand up and leave the room. Jax pulls out his pack of smokes and heads outside. Jax exits to the patio, and Doctor Lassen follows, addressing Jax: "Jax, are you willing to have our one-on-one now?"

"Can you deal with the smoke?" Both sit.

"Yes"

"Well then, the floor is yours, Doc!"

They both sit on the bench, and the doctor pulls out her notepad.

"So, Jax, let's talk about your childhood. You haven't talked at all about your past. We seem to believe that you are hiding it."

"My childhood hasn't been the issue on why I'm here, plus no one has really asked me."

"Nevertheless, Jax, start at birth and up to when you joined the Marines."

"I need a drink." Jax lights another cigarette and places his elbow on his knees. "I was born in Los Angeles, California, to a drug addict. She had a daughter already that was two, and her dad made her give me away. She went on to have four more kids. Another boy she kept, the third boy she put for adoption, and then she kept two more girls. I bounced from foster home to foster home. CPA would see bruises and move me. When I hit twelve, my adoptive parents got me and adopted me. They adopted another boy, but gave him up, so I thought they would do the same thing to me. So I lived in fear until I joined the Marines. My adoptive parents loved me a lot. Mom was my backbone. Dad loved to beat me and make me practice basketball. It wasn't until before his death in 2015, that I saw his soft side, and we made up. My mom died from diabetes in 2008. So they are both gone. End of story."

"Wow, Jax I'm so proud of you. That's the most you have ever said to me! I'm so happy; thank you for trusting me with that story."

"Sure."

"Your record does say forty-two foster homes back and forth from 1981–1993."

"So you know my history.

"We have paperwork but not your side of things. So families abused you? Physically? Sexually? Emotionally?"

Jax leans back rubs his head. "All three; can we drop this now?"

"Jax, it wasn't your fault. You never did anything wrong. You were innocent, and they took that away."

"Just stop, Doctor."

"Jax, it was not your fault."

"Stop. Please."

"Jax, look at me." Dr. Lassen moves closer to Jax and repeats herself again. Jax is getting red, and his forehead and hands sweat profusely. "Jax, it's not your fault.

Jax breaks down and starts crying. He drops his cigarette and cups his face with his hands and sobs uncontrollably. Dr. Lassen places one hand on Jax shoulder as he cries harder.

The Ex-wives: Day 30

"Jax, why is it I always find you smoking when it's time for our one-on-ones?"

Dr. Eve Lassen jokes with Jax as she saunters out onto the patio. Although Jax has Shanna, he can always appreciate a beautiful woman. Jax has always been a ladies' man—he has always had a girlfriend or wife in his later years.

And that's what Dr. Lassen wants to cover today with Jax. Jax is thirty-six with four children and three ex-wives. He is an overachiever, to say the least. He says he falls in love too easily, but there are deeper issues that need to be addressed, but that takes more time to dig in. So the basics will be a start of his trilogy of wives.

The doc sits down in her usual seat across from Jax, crosses her legs, and pops the cap off her pen and looks at Jax.

"So, Doc, what's the gut-wrenching topic of the day?"

She laughs and starts writing in her pad.

"That's not fair, Doc. I haven't even said anything yet."

She laughs and turns her pad around displaying what she wrote.

Jax turns ghost-white. "*Fuck me*!"

The paper reads:

Ex Wife #1

Ex Wife #2

Ex Wife #3

"Doc, I'm not even sure how to go about talking about them."

"Jax, start out with who they were. I'm not looking to dig in too deep, but I'd like to see what you come up with on the surface."

"Okay."

Jax lights up a cigarette, looks at Dr. Lassen, and smiles while shaking his head. Jax looks up at the sky. It's a beautiful fall day with only a few clouds in the chill sky.

"It was early 2000s, and I came home to see my parents. And by luck I met Jen at Starbucks in Morgan

Hill. I was walking in, our hands touched and eyes connected, and at the time she had green contacts in and red hair. I was a goner. I had leave for thirty days. So I spent every day in that Starbucks until I finally got the nerve to ask her out. It was a whirlwind romance. But I got caught in some lies, and she left me. Few months later she hit me up and was pregnant. I quickly married her, and we had Kaylen. Two years later, we had Parker. I was always gone and not meeting her needs as a husband, but what do you expect, marrying a Marine?

"Shortly after, I met Candy. Gorgeous from head to toe, with the biggest heart. We married in Vegas at the Luxor, and Nick passed away. Then Susie committed suicide, and we got Ava, who was the biggest blessing in the world. But Candy cheated. I wasn't honest with her and kept deploying, and she left me before the end of the first year."

"Why the dishonesty, Jax?"

"I was afraid to get in trouble so I'd tell a white lie that would snowball and kick my ass."

"Did you break that habit?"

"Yes, Ivory got me out of that.

"Tell me about her."

"Ivory did a number on me but in a good way. I got "saved" when I was with Candy but didn't walk the walk of a Christian until I fell in love with Ivory. I had just retired and moved back to Gilroy, California. I partied rather hard that night. The next day, me and Steve went to a friend's kid's birthday party. I had to pound a few beers to get rid of my hangover. Then there she was.

"Golden blonde hair and blue eyes that could melt an iceberg. Her smile softened my hard heart that night. It was like finding a fallen angel. She was wearing wings, too, so it made it seem like God directed me to her. We went out after the party and met up at a ritual bonfire the gang had on Saturday nights. Once intoxicated, Steven and I wanted food and headed to Denny's, so I asked her to join us.

"Everyone knows that moment they fell in love and when, where, and why it happened. I'm no different. While sitting at Denny's, Ivory reached across the table and put her fork into my country potatoes. She didn't even ask, and I didn't even care. She smiled at me, and I was a goner. We dated about six months and she got pregnant and we got married. It unfortunately didn't last due to my absences once again, along with other things like finances and normal couple issues."

"What's your new girlfriend think of all of this?"

"I'm not sure, but she stands by me. We don't have your typical relationship right now."

"How do you mean?"

Jax lights up another cigarette and continues.

"We have been best friends for nine years. And the night I committed myself, we kissed for the first time. So we haven't ever gone on a date yet."

"Where do you see things going?"

"She is the one. I never felt like this. She will be my forever."

"I think that's very positive thinking. But do you think you rush things with women?"

"Yes, I have in the past. But this has been nine years in the making."

"Very good session, Jax. We will dig deeper on another session."

The First Cut Is the Deepest: Day 40

Once again Jax finds himself first to show up to group. He sits in his usual spot with his back against the wall, facing the windows and still in view of all the exits. Jax hasn't liked the groups due to the overwhelming fact that Dr. Mendoza makes him tear up every damn time. One by one, patients file in, and like always, Dr. Mendoza is late and last to take his seat.

Today Jax feels like shit. He has been through hell in this MHU and encountered feelings and emotions he hasn't felt in years. But more than that he feels the need to talk, which is unusual since it's group.

"Okay, group, today we will go around the room and talk about pain. But not just normal pain but pain we create or is self-inflicted."

Jax leans back and tilts his head back and sighs. He looks over to the Doc and tosses him a "you bastard" look.

"Jax, since you seem to not be happy with this topic, you will start us off.

"Fuck that, why do you always pick on me?"

"Jax, I am not picking on you. Maybe you won't toss a dirty look at me next time."

"Isn't that unprofessional of you?"

"You're a Marine not a Cub Scout, Jax. Suck it up."

"Did you have to pull the Marine card?"

"Yes, sir!"

Jax places his face in his hands.

"What kind of pain, Doc?"

"The pain, Jax, of what have you done to yourself? What left the biggest hole in your soul?"

Jax looks at the Doc and knows exactly what he means. He has been transported back to high school in his mind. Jax has started to sweat, and he looks around the group.

He sees everyone's eyes on him. He has never shared in group, ever! He usually leaves right before his turn or has some excuse on why he can't share.

"Look, I don't group share."

"Jax, looks like today we change that."

Jax nervously adjusts himself in the chair. He starts to fidget with his sweater's zipper.

"I was sixteen. I had been adopted for four years at this point. The beatings from my dad were at their high."

"Jax, before you continue, I have to report an abuse, physically or sexually."

"He's dead; go for it."

"Oh, I'm sorry."

"You gonna fucking listen now, Doc?"

"Yes."

Jax leans back and feels his chest as if his wounds have just been made. "My dad used to make me practice shooting baskets and dribbling until my fingers were raw. By that time he was massively drunk. Once I was done and packed up the gear, I'd hurry inside. Usually he would be hitting my mom first. Then I'd say something to distract him and draw his beatings to me.

"At sixteen, I was six foot, 200 pounds, yet I couldn't stand up for myself. I was too afraid to be sent back to foster care. After a busted lip and black eye, I'd be sent to bed without dinner."

"Once in my room, I'd cry and bandage myself up with a first aid kit my mom bought me. That night started a habit I never thought was possible.

I'd pull out my candle and light it. I sat here bleeding and crying. Just staring at the flame. Next to the candle was a pinewood derby car I was working on. On top of it was the razor blade. I sat there now thinking about that razor blade. I grabbed it and felt how sharp it was. My thought process started to slip into the darkness as I felt the tip of the blade.

"I started piecing together a plan. Bouncing from flame to blade back to the flame. I put the tip of the blade into the flame. I heated it until it glowed a bright yellow. I took off my shirt and sat there with the blade next to my skin. The heat was so intense.

"I wasn't sure what to do. I'd sit there for the next hour or so heating and reheating the blade and hovering above the skin."

Jax was in another time, but the more and more he talked, he could hear the gasps from his small captivated group.

"I reheated the blade and was crying and started thinking about the beating I just took. I took that blade and stabbed it into my chest. I can still smell my flesh burning. I cried out loud, and the heat cauterized the wound, so there wasn't too much blood. But for the first time, "life pain" disappeared. I felt free. So every night for the next couple years, I'd do the same thing over and over. I filled up my chest with little scars and looked like a battlefield."

Jax wipes away his tears and sniffles the snot back into his brain.

"Jax do you still have the scars?"

"I tattooed my chest to hide the shame I felt for cutting."

Jax removes his shirt and walks up close to Dr. Mendoza and through the ink you can see the remains of cuts all over his chest; hundreds of half-inch cuts riddle Jax's chest.

"Jax, the step you just took is amazing. I am proud of you."

Dr. Mendoza claps, and the group all stands and slaps and walks toward Jax and look at his chest. One woman who was in the Marines as well walks up and hugs Jax. She then lifts her shirt up. Right below her breasts she reveals to Jax her cuts. Jax loses it and starts balling. He wraps his arms around her, and they embrace and cry into each other's souls. A true freeing moment.

"Okay, group, let's take a short ten-minute break and refresh ourselves."

Everyone files out except Jax and the woman.

"It's okay. You're okay," Jax says. She silently nods her head.

"You ever need me, I'm here for you, sister."

She nods again. She turns and walks out, and Jax stands there and wipes his tears for the cutting. The first cut may have been the deepest, but the last cut has been healed deep in his soul.

The Exit Plan Day 44

In Doctor Robertson's office, Dr. Robertson, Dr. Lassen, and Dr. Mendoza have a final meeting regarding Jax's treatment.

Dr. Robertson began. "So our next case is SSgt Jax Guerra. Dr. Mendoza, group status please?"

"He takes full participation in groups and now is rather funny."

"Excellent. Doctor Lassen, how are the one-on-ones going?"

"I need a lot more one-on-one with Jax. The trauma he has seen just as a boy is horrific, and the teen years into adulthood play like a Greek tragedy."

Dr. Robertson answered, "That's too bad. I recommended outpatient with Dr. Lassen as well as group meetings twice a week."

The others agreed.

Dr. Robertson continued, "We will release SSgt Jax Guerra as planned tomorrow morning. Dr. Lassen, please inform SSgt to make pickup arrangements."

"Yes, Doctor." Doctor Lassen walks down the hall and knocks on Jax's door.

"Hey Doc, am I late or something?"

Dr. Lassen laughs, "No, Jax. Make a phone call, SSgt. You'll be released at 7 a.m. tomorrow. Please have a ride ready." The doctor shakes Jax's hand and leaves the room.

Now, Jax is sneaky, so he has plotted a plan to surprise Shanna. He rushes to the phone and calls William and lets him know to pick him up at 7 a.m. Next he dials Shanna.

He says, "Hey, baby."

"Hey, my love. We are busy, so I have to be fast. I'm sorry."

"Okay, babe. Tomorrow I'm out at 3 p.m. William will pick you up at 2:30 p.m."

"Awesome! I love you! See you soon, baby!"

"Bye, Banana."

The Exit and the Forever

Six a.m. and Jax is all packed and ready to bust out of this joint. All that's left is to do is eat chow and take pills from Nurse Ratchette one last time.

Santos left a few days prior, so his main farewell is done, but he got his number to stay in touch. Plus he is only out of Morgan Hill, so it's not too far away.

Jax grabs his stuff and places it at the front of the chow hall. Jax walks into the chow hall, and Nurse Ratchette has his food and pills in hand. Nurse Mariah walks in, gives him his discharge paperwork, kisses him on the cheek, and hugs Jax. Then she walks away as she sheds a tear for his recovery.

Jax takes his pills and food and sits down. Astonishingly enough, Nurse Ratchette mutters, "See you later, Marine," and walks away. Another nurse walks in, asks his name, and once she verifies him, she hands him his personal property. Jax quickly eats as his texts are pouring in since his phone has been off for forty-five days. Jax finishes half his food and heads out the ten doors it takes to leave the hospital.

Jax stands looking around like he hasn't been outside for years. William texts back with, "5 min out." So Jax lights up a cigarette and sits on a bench on the side of the pickup circle. William pulls up, and Jax tosses his bags in the back of Will's truck. Jax cracks open the door and, as usual, trash falls out—cigarette packs and empty Red Bull cans. Jax hops in, and they commence their traditional handshake and hug.

"You ready for this?"

"Yes, Kaylie is ready with all her friends like you requested—four trucks full, ten girls—ten giggly, annoying girls."

"Good. Let's go to Jared and then to the florist off Pomoroy."

"You got it, bro. We really fucking missed you, man."

After a grueling jewelry store run and hitting three florists for the right flowers, they are finally done, and they received a text, saying that all the girls are downtown and ready.

It's 2:15 p.m., and Will files into the coffee shop and gets his coffee and tells Shanna she has twenty minutes until they leave.

"What's that sneaky smile about, William?"

"Not sneaky, just gassy."

William picks a seat, so he can watch it all go down and begins recording.

William texts Kaylie, and she comes walking in with a fully bloomed sunflower. Shanna sees Kaylie and gasps. She knows something is up.

"I love you, Shanna."

Kaylie hands her the sunflower and sits by William. Shanna walks around the counter as the next girl comes in.

"He loves his Banana."

She hands Shanna the sunflower. Shanna starts to tear as she stands in front of her pickup window. Girl after girl comes in and hands her a sunflower.

"He has missed his Banana."

"Never will he leave his Banana."

The final flower walks in; attached to the flower is Ava.

"My daddy loves you like he loves cake."

Shanna laughs and snorts to that. All the flowers have been delivered, and Shanna walk to the front door. She looks left and right and doesn't see Jax. All of a sudden behind her she hears him.

"Banana."

Shanna turns around, hand covering her mouth, as tears flow like Niagara Falls. She takes steps toward Jax and is trying to hold back her crying. But she is failing. Shanna gets within steps from Jax. Jax takes the final few steps and grabs her left hand. With tears in his eyes, Jax begins his speech.

"Banana, I've been blinded. Blinded by my ego, pride, and other women who have tried to keep you out of my life. And for nine years you have stood by and fought tooth and nail to stay in my life and supported all my decisions and mistakes. For nine years you loved me and waited for this moment. When our love connected I just had to have a mental breakdown, and our love got put on hold again. You called me, you answered my calls, visited me, and gave me 110 percent. You helped with my kids and showed them love as a mother when you didn't have to."

William, still recording, wipes a tear.

"You have become a second mom to them, and they love and respect you like I do. You accept me for my good, my bad, and my ugly. I accept you the same. And for all this, I can't ignore it anymore."

Jax gets down on one knee and pulls out a two-carat yellow diamond with white diamonds as pedals of a sunflower ring.

"Shanna, will you marry me?"

"Yes."

Shanna barely could say it but got it out. Sobs and tears flow as Jax stands up as the coffee shop erupts in clapping and cheering.

Jax and Shanna embrace and kiss, and the world fades away. After a few minutes they release their embrace, and Kaylie walks up.

"Kaylie, I love you! I heard you were an adult while I was away, and you stepped up when I needed you to. I'm very proud of you."

"Thanks, Daddy, I love you, too."

Jax hugs his daughter and Ava comes running up and hugs them both.

"Okay, everyone, let's go eat. I'm done with hospital food."

Kaylie looks to Shanna.

"Momma, can I ride with you?"

Shanna's face lights up, and she looks over to Jax. Jax's jaw is open and on the floor.

"Yes, honey, you can."

Jax still looks shocked at what he just heard. He smiles at Shanna, and she smiles back, and he tosses her his famous wink. Shanna cracks up and blushes.

"I miss Mommy and Daddy, but I'm glad you're my daddy now."

"I am very happy you're my daughter now, too, baby girl."

Jax picks her up and hugs her and kisses her cheek.

For a second, explosions sound off and gunshots fire off, but this time Jax is medicated and knows they aren't real, and he continues out the door.

The Love We Make

After a big Italian dinner at Maggiano's everyone piles back into their cars, ready for a food coma. They all head back to Jax's Campbell home.

When they arrive, Jen is already impatiently waiting at the front curb. The kids jump out of the cars and surround their dad, asking to stay longer. William passes them all and heads straight for the garage fridge for the beers.

Jax explains it's not his weekend and having them was a special circumstance. They all kiss and hug their dad and trade "I love yous." They all pile into Jen's minivan.

William comes back outside and waves, half-assed, with a handful of beer bottles. He opens each one with his belt buckle. Yes, he drinks a lot. Jax and Shanna take a beer from Williams. Williams raises his beer.

"Fine day y'all." Jax and Shanna raise theirs as well.

"Salude."

"Cheers."

They all tap bottles.

"Will . . ."

William interrupts Jax.

"I know, time for me to go."

They all laugh, and William slams his beer down his throat and tosses his bottle in the bed of his truck.

Jax slyly takes Shanna by the hand as they wave bye to William. Jax leans in and kisses Shanna on the cheek.

"Want to come in, Banana?"

"*Duh!*"

They both chuckle, and Jax leads her into the house while never losing eye contact.

"Apple whiskey?"

"Of course."

"Uno?"

"Heck yeah."

"Perfect." Jax picks up Shanna and carries her over the threshold.

"Jax, what are you doing?"

"Practicing," he says with a sly smile.

They realize after a brief few minutes that "us" feels natural and fits like a glove.

Jax picks up a new bottle of apple whiskey and two glasses. Shanna plops down on the couch and grabs the Uno deck on the coffee table.

Jax pours them a half glass of whiskey, hers over ice and his straight up. While Shanna shuffles the Uno deck, Jax quietly turn his stereo on and puts Shanna's favorite song on. Chris Stapleton's "Tennessee Whiskey" softly plays.

Shanna stops, leans back, closes her eyes, and moans. Jax walks over to Shanna, reaches down and grabs her hand, pulls her up, and holds her tight to his body. Her face turns red as though she had drunk all the whiskey already.

Jax places her arms on his shoulders, and he softly wraps his arms around her waist and pulls her in tight so she feels all of his body.

They start to spin slowly. Shanna lays her head on Jax's chest, and he feels her breath and heartbeat.

Jax reaches up and gently removes the hair away from her face, placing his hand on the side of her face so that she knows he wants to kiss her. She looks up, and their eyes connect. Time stand still. Jax leans in, and their lips barely touch. Jax slides his tongue across her bottom lip. Breathing heavily, they try to catch their breath. Shanna extends her tongue into Jax's mouth. Their lips collide as their tongues dance.

Jax reaches up Shanna's dress and pulls her close again by both hands, grabbing a handful of ass.

"Whiskey and Uno first, Marine. You can't have me just yet."

Jax pulls Shanna in and goes in like he is going to kiss her and licks the side of her face.

"Oh Jax, you dick!"

Jax just laughs and grabs his whiskey and takes a swig.

But Jax isn't giving up that easily. As they sit down on the couch, Jax reaches under the couch and pulls out Shanna's favorite lotion that she uses every day after work. It's the most favorite thing of her day besides Jax and his flirting.

Shanna looks at Jax, shocked. Jax grabs both of her legs and places her feet in his lap.

"Jax, how did you know?"

"Banana, I pay attention more than you think."

Shanna gasps and starts to tear up, for she knows that Jax for sure is *the one*. No one ever massaged her feet and calves before.

Jax works on her feet and moves up to her calves. He gets up to her knees, but when he tries to go higher, Shanna said, "Hands below the knees, Marine. Nice try."

Jax keeps going and notices her eyes have closed, and she is biting her bottom lip. So he tries to go above the knees. This time she didn't stop him. After working on her thighs, he moves his hands higher. As her dress goes up, he sees she is not wearing any panties. He forgot she never wears them. Jax is hard as a rock and ready to roll.

Jax places his hands under her and lifts her up. She wraps her legs around him. He pulls her closer and digs his crotch into hers.

They kiss furiously in a mass heat of passion. Jax grips her tight and takes four steps to his bedroom and enters his hallway. He takes one more step and slams Shanna's elbow into the corner of the wall.

"Damn it"

"Shit, Banana, I'm sorry."

They both laugh, and she wraps her arms around Jax's neck and starts kissing his ear lobe and neck with some added bites and tongue.

"Fuck, that was almost some *Notebook*-type shit."

"I love you, Marine."

"I love you to the moon and back." Jax takes the final steps into the bedroom.

Jax places Shanna down in front of the bed. He steps in closer to her and kisses her lips. He reaches up behind her and unzips her dress, and it falls to the floor. He unclasps her bra.

Shanna reaches and grabs Jax's shirt and pulls it off. She undoes his belt, and his pants fall to the floor. He takes off his boxer briefs. Jax stands there hard and pulsating, and Shanna is literally dripping wet.

Jax steps in and slides his cock across her wet lips. He picks her up and lays her down. He starts kissing her as he slides deep inside her and says "I love you" as he does.

Jax is treating her as if she is his queen and like he opened the best Christmas present ever. They whisper back and forth, "I love you."

The love we make tells our future. It extends life moment by moment, touch by touch, thrust by thrust.

To Jax and Shanna, time has stopped, and the world stopped spinning. Cupid said, "Fuck it," and quit his job since he couldn't have created such a love. Shakespeare turned in his grave because not even he could write about a love this great.

Epilogue
October 1, 2017

Bam—Jax's internal clock wakes him up. An exhausting yet invigorating night wore him out. He rolls over to see Shanna lying there beside him. Both are still nude from the night's festivities. Jax takes his hand and softly touches the side of Shanna's face. She stirs a bit but falls back to sleep.

Jax gets up, and rather than his normal routine, he decides to make Shanna a quick breakfast in bed before work.

Jax gets a few eggs and bacon out of the fridge and a potato from the counter. Jax turns on his stove plate, cracks the eggs in a bowl, and mixes them with some cheese and milk. He chops the potato and tosses in all on the stove plate. While the potatoes are going, he feed four oranges into the juicer. Ten minutes into the cooking, Shanna makes her first appearance. And like any amazing woman she arrived in proper fashion. Hair up in a ponytail, Jax's shirt, and panties. Nothing else could ever be as sexy as a woman in her man's button-up shirt from the night before.

She stands leaning on the kitchen door frame. Jax walks up, leans in, and kisses her softly on the forehead and then her lips. He hugs her, and they embrace with light sighs of ecstasy.

Jax greeted her, "Good morning, *mi amour.*"

"Happy birthday, my love."

"Thanks, baby. Now go back to bed. I'll be in there in five minutes."

Shanna smiles and returns back to bed. Within five minutes, Jax returns to the bedroom with Shanna's breakfast. When he enters he arrives to see Shanna naked in the center of the bed waiting. He looks at Shanna and says, "Happy birthday to *me*."

Shanna giggles, and Jax puts the food down and jumps back into bed.

Later That Night

Jax stands proud, for it is thirty-six years to the day he was born, and now he gazes into the never-ending expanse of the ocean. He holds two beers and places them on the railing in front of him. Jax pulls out his pack of cigarettes, places one in his mouth, and lights it. Jax takes his lighter and cracks open both beers and sets one back on the railing. He lifts his beer and exhales smoke.

"For you, Coleman. And also to every man, woman, and child, soldier, marine, airman, and seaman"—Jax chuckles—"who never made it home. To us who came home and are still stuck in that giant sandbox of shit. This is for you. We all live and die; we sweat and bleed. We toss and turn night after night. The days and night fueled with gunpowder and glory are over, and the lust we share for it plagues our souls without it. We are trained to kill and trained to die before dishonor. This is for us, that we may live again, that we may love again, that we may fight not for glory, but for peace of mind that what we once were and who we once were does not predict our death but gives foundation to our future."

Jax takes a drink of beer. A hand reaches up and touches Jax shoulder.

"You know, Jax, They have AA in Santa Cruz." Dusty laughs as he hands Jax his truck keys. Jax laughs and replies, "Very true but why spend $20 when you cost a couple beers?" Both of them concur with a short grunt and head nod and stare off out into the ocean. Dusty, with an inquisitive look on his face says, "Jax, I think they wrote a song about this."

"This isn't a movie, Dusty." They both chuckle at the same time.

"I'm gonna sit right here at the end of this pier and watch the sun set disappear and drink a beer."

Shanna walks up from behind them, takes a beer out of the six pack, and opens it with a twist. Both Jax and Dusty look at her with amazement.

"What, they twist off, boys."

Shanna raises her beer.

"Until Valhalla?"

"Until Valhalla!" they responded in a chant.

Dusty and Shanna start walking away, and with his beer still raised, Jax says one last thing. "We will fight, we will kick, and we will not give in to the wars within." He takes one last sip, places the beer down, and walks away.

Bibliography

Luke Bryan, "Drink a beer", track 6 on Crash my Party, Liberty Records, 2013, compact disc.

Photo Section

A.J. Perrish, San Francisco Ca.
@tat2devinvphotography

A.J. Perrish, Tracy Ca.
@tat2devinvphotography

A.J. Perrish, Tracy Ca.
@tat2devinvphotography

A.J. Perrish, Tracy Ca.
@tat2devinvphotography

A.J. Perrish, Old Sacramento Ca.
@tat2devinvphotography

2000 With Mom and Dad Before leaving for the Marines.
I miss you both.

A.J. Perrish , Tracy Ca.
@tat2devinvphotography

A.J. Perrish , Tracy Ca.
@tat2devinvphotography

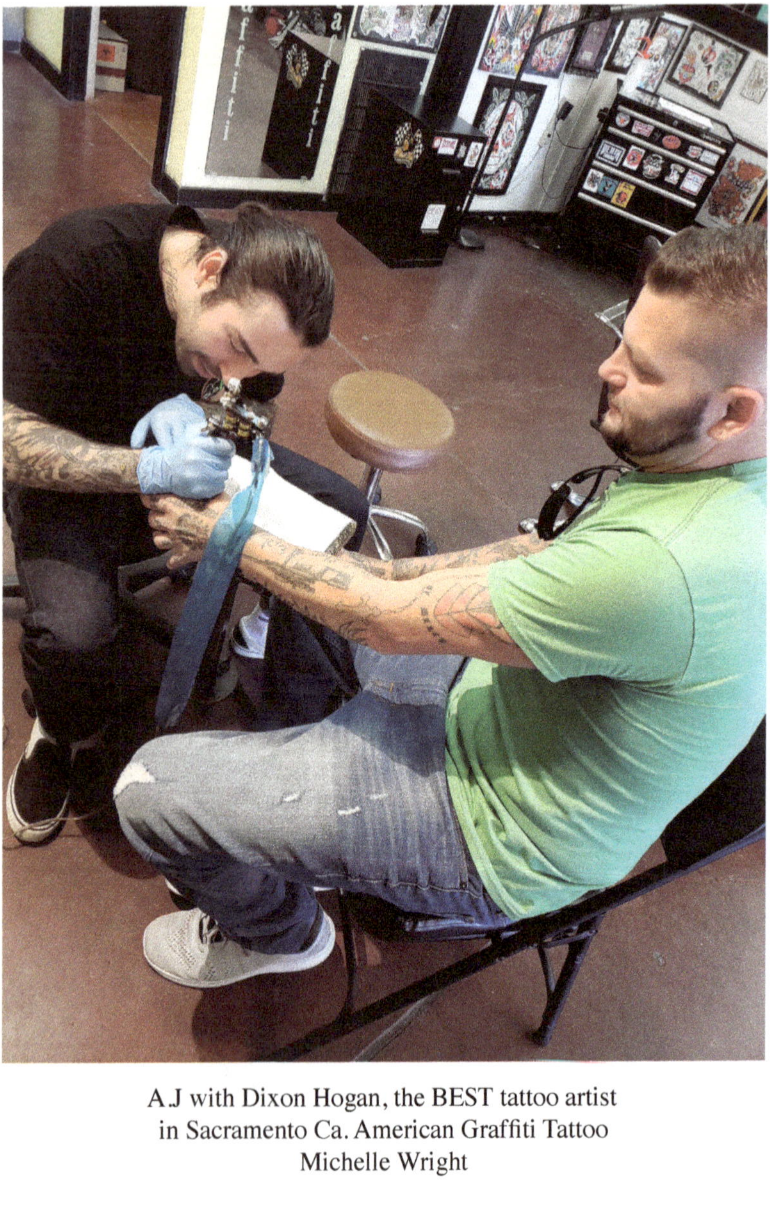

A.J with Dixon Hogan, the BEST tattoo artist
in Sacramento Ca. American Graffiti Tattoo
Michelle Wright

Mr. Carlyle , Teacher I happen to run into in Sacramento at the Hyatt Regency. The teacher who never gave up on me.

A.J. Perrish, Old Sacramento Ca.

A.J. Perrish, Old Sacramento Ca.

A.J. Perrish, Sacramento Ca.

A.J. Perrish, Sacramento Ca.

SWOP Ball with Michelle

SWOP Ball with Michelle

A.J. Perrish, Tracy Ca.
@tat2devinvphotography

A.J. Perrish, Tracy Ca.
@tat2devinvphotography

A.J. Perrish, Tracy Ca.
@tat2devinvphotography

A.J. Perrish and Katherine Robertson, San Francisco Ca.
@tat2devinvphotography

A.J. Perrish and Katherine Robertson, San Francisco Ca.
@tat2devinvphotography

A.J. Perrish, San Francisco Ca.
@tat2devinvphotography

A.J. Perrish and Katherine Robertson, San Francisco Ca.
@tat2devinvphotography

A.J. Perrish and Katherine Robertson, San Francisco Ca.
@tat2devinvphotography

A.J. Perrish and Katherine Robertson, San Francisco Ca.
@tat2devinvphotography

A.J. Perrish's Birthday party

A.J. Perrish's Birthday party

A.J. with his youngest son Lucas

A.J. with his youngest son Lucas

A.J. Perrish and Katherine Robertson, San Francisco Ca.
@tat2devinvphotography

A.J. Culture photoshoot

A.J. Culture photoshoot

A.J. Perrish and Katherine Robertson, San Francisco Ca.
@tat2devinvphotography

A.J. Perrish, San Francisco Ca.
@tat2devinvphotography

A.J. Perrish and Katherine Robertson, San Francisco Ca.
@tat2devinvphotography

A.J. Perrish, Tracy Ca.
@tat2devinvphotography

A.J. and Michelle first dance

Sometimes you have to bribe Santa!
@tat2devinvphotography

Have to end with a selfie and thank you all for buying this book.
See you in the next book pages! LOVE – A.J.

Marshaun Olaniyan
LIFE & RELATIONSHIP STRATEGIST I KEYNOTE SPEAKER
Marshaun Olaniyan is a certified Life & Relationship Strategist, transformational coach, keynote speaker and author of her first book "Twenty Ways To Create An Awesome Love Story," releasing in April 2019. Marshaun's mission is to decrease the divorce rate while simultaneously increasing the marriage rate by supplying men and women with the strategies and tools to implement in their relationship. She shares honest, straightforward, thought-provoking life experiences and advice.
1-on-1 Coaching
Group Coaching
Online Courses
For bookings and pre-orders email:
marshaun@marshaunolaniyan.com

PEAK PERFORMANCE THROUGH SUCCESS MASTERY
Achieve positive outcomes by using Guided Visualizaton.
Michael Casselberry RN empowers veterans to reach their Peak Performance in areas that matter most to them. We teach them through the power of relaxation how to use the power of their mind to use past positive performances to create new positive realities.
An initial conversation helps to establish where they are in life currently and where they would like to be. Through continued discussion, we determine what a positive outcome is and the significance it has on their lives.
By learning to Master Success, a person can achieve their Peak Performance.
CALL FOR A FREE CONSULTATION
619.491.7011

RUCKPACK®
COMBAT NUTRITION
RUCKPACK.COM
FROM OUR BATTLEFIELD TO YOURS
RUCKPACK FUELS VICTORIES.
RUCKPACK
FOCUS SHOT
RUCKPACK IS COMBAT NUTRITION.
FOR EVERY BATTLE.
A VETERAN OWNED AND OPERATED COMPANY
LEARN MORE AT WWW.RUCKPACK.COM

Lightning Source UK Ltd.
Milton Keynes UK
UKHW020611210219
337696UK00002B/2/P

9 781545 662632